125 best
ground
meat recipes

125 best
ground
meat recipes

ILANA SIMON

Robert
ROSE

125 Best Ground Meat Recipes
Text copyright © 2003 Ilana Simon
Photographs copyright © 2003 Robert Rose Inc.

For complete cataloguing information, see page 187.

Disclaimer
The recipes in this book have been carefully tested by our kitchen and our tasters. To the best of our knowledge, they are safe and nutritious for ordinary use and users. For those people with food or other allergies, or who have special food requirements or health issues, please read the suggested contents of each recipe carefully and determine whether or not they may create a problem for you. All recipes are used at the risk of the consumer.

We cannot be responsible for any hazards, loss or damage that may occur as a result of any recipe use.

For those with special needs, allergies, requirements or health problems, in the event of any doubt, please contact your medical adviser prior to the use of any recipe.

Design & Production: PageWave Graphics Inc.
Editor: Carol Sherman
Copy Editor: Julia Armstrong
Recipe Tester: Jennifer MacKenzie
Photography: Mark T. Shapiro
Food Stylist: Kate Bush
Props Stylist: Charlene Erricson
Color Scans: Colour Technologies

The publisher and author wish to express their appreciation to the following supplier of props used in the food photography:

FLATWARE
Gourmet Settings Inc.
245 West Beaver Creek Rd., Unit 10
Richmond Hill, Ontario, L4B 1L1
Tel: 1-800-551-2649
www.gourmetsettings.com

Cover Image: Mexican Chicken Casserole (see recipe, page 94)

We acknowledge the financial support of the Government of Canada through the Book Publishing Industry Development Program (BPIDP) for our publishing activities.

Published by: Robert Rose Inc.
120 Eglinton Ave. E., Suite 800, Toronto, Ontario, Canada M4P 1E2
Tel: (416) 322-6552 Fax: (416) 322-6936

Printed in Canada
1 2 3 4 5 6 7   GP   09 08 07 06 05 04 03

Contents

Acknowledgments

Writing a cookbook is always a team effort. First, I want to thank my home team: my husband, Ari Marantz, and my sons, Jesse and Evan. I couldn't have done it without your support and great taste-testing sensibilities. Thank you for your good-natured sampling of ground meat dishes on a daily basis for months on end, and for your valuable insights into making every recipe great!

Next, hats off to Canada's eminent cookbook publisher, Bob Dees, who always has his pulse on the latest palate pleaser. It's been a delight working with you again.

Three cheers to the awesome creative team: editor Carol Sherman, a sharp, scrupulous editor who is also understanding and kind; Andrew Smith, Joseph Gisini, Kevin Cockburn and Daniella Zanchetta of PageWave Graphics for the outstanding book design and layout; and recipe tester Jennifer MacKenzie and copy editor Julia Armstrong for catching all the little things that helped make my recipes even better. And to the talented trio of food stylist Kate Bush, props stylist Charlene Erricson and food photographer Mark Shapiro, I extend my gratitude for enhancing the cookbook with fabulous photography.

Many people have helped bring this project to fruition. I am grateful to recipe tester and home economist Cheryl Warkentin and to my friends and family for their invaluable input.

Special thanks to my mother-in-law, Brenda Marantz, for all her vegetarian wisdom, and to my mom, Betty Simon, and my sisters, Anna-Gail, Sherrill and Debbie, for their confidence in all of my endeavors.

Introduction

◆━━━━━━━━━━━━━━━━━━━━━━━━━━━━━━━━━━━━

Ground meat may very well be the quintessential North American food ingredient. It's inexpensive, versatile, accessible, convenient, reliable, and we can't seem to get enough of it! While ground beef still wins the popularity contest, more consumers are turning to ground chicken and ground turkey as lower-fat options. As well, ground pork, ground lamb, ground veal and vegetarian ground "beef" replacement prevail as excellent choices for specific dishes and present yet another mealtime alternative.

Like many of you, I depend on ground beef a couple of times a week to feed my family of four, which includes two growing boys — a teenager and an adolescent. They never tire of traditional *Spaghetti and Meatballs*, *Tacos* or *Classic Lasagna*, but they are also game to check out new takes on old favorites, such as *Stuffed Turkey Meat Loaf*, *Veal and Potato Pie* and *Mango Chicken Meatballs*. And during the months I spent testing recipes for this book, they loved the fact that Middle Eastern, Asian, Greek, Italian and other ethnic-inspired ground meat dishes meant they never had a chance to "get bored." And that's the beauty of ground meat: its appeal is universal, and the creative possibilities are endless.

As a staple ingredient, ground meat shines equally bright as the basis of a quick weeknight meal and as entertaining fare. It is suited to speedy preparation methods, such as sautéing for a skillet main event, combining everything for a one-dish meal or partnering with a boiled pot of pasta. As well, ground meat is easily taken up a notch for elegant entrées, such as *Lamb Moussaka* and *Spinach and Beef Strudel*, or for stylish appetizers, such as *Chicken and Wild Mushroom Bundles* and *Jerk Puffs*. It serves just as well as the starting point for a potluck dinner contribution, a welcome-to-the-neighborhood offering or a portable repast to pack for the cottage.

Savvy consumers who purchase ground meat in bulk (when it's on sale!) and freeze it in handy portions for later use will value my wide selection of both traditional and contemporary ground meat recipes. Likewise, since most of us rely on certain prepared products, I've incorporated many of today's convenience ingredients, such as canned chicken broth, pasta sauce, canned beans, dried herbs and ready-to-use pastry, to make putting dinner on the table even easier. However, when you have the time, and inclination, you'll be delighted to try your hand at make-from-scratch recipes for *Calzones* and *Sausage Rolls* or more labor-intensive (but well worth the effort) *Stuffed Grape Leaves*, *Egg Rolls* and *Curried Chicken Tartlets*.

Ground meat's adaptability means you can enjoy barbecued *Teriyaki Chicken Burgers* or *Salsa Hamburgers* in the summer, then piquant *Chipotle Beef Chili* and homey *Meatball and Rigatoni Stew* in the fall. Simmering *Italian Wedding Soup* and traditional *Tourtière* provide perfect cool-weather cuisine. *Sausage and Ricotta Manicotti Shells*, *Meat Samosas* and *Pastitsio* present superlative spring entertaining ideas. Meanwhile, all year long, you'll want to savor such simple one-dish meals as *Mexican Chicken Casserole*, *Scalloped Potato Meat Loaf* and *Sweet-and-Sour Meatballs*.

In today's busy world, where parents juggle demanding work responsibilities and their family's hectic extracurricular schedules, preparing healthful, homemade meals is a challenge. I know what it's like trying to get a well-balanced dinner on the table before hockey practices, swimming classes or piano lessons — never mind when baseball and soccer season start! I've included many express entrées for just such occasions: *Ground Turkey Sloppy Joes*, *Three-Cheese Penne Hamburger Skillet*, *Taco Salad*, *Pantry Chow Mein*, *Quick Ground Veal and Chickpea Soup* and *Cheeseburger Pie*, to name a few. These recipes require minimal preparation time, incorporate healthy fresh vegetables and modest amounts of fat, but are satisfying and delicious. What more could you ask for?

One of my greatest pleasures in writing **125 Best Ground Meat Recipes** was the opportunity to share my family's favorite hearty ground meat recipes — *Can't Miss Chili*, *Shepherd's Pie*, *Stuffed Peppers* — and I hope they will become stand-bys in your household as well.

Nothing replaces the joy of home cooking. And despite our frenzied lives, taking the time to prepare a meal reaps its own set of rewards, including your family's appreciation and a feel-good sense of personal accomplishment. Cooking enhances family life by bringing everyone to the table at mealtime to partake of a time-honored tradition.

Aside from being economical, practical and quick to prepare, ground meat also affords the opportunity for big-batch cooking and freezing, advance preparation and the mouth-watering aromas that waft through your kitchen as you prepare a simmering stew or pasta bake.

So here's to discovering — or rediscovering — all varieties of ground meat as you arm yourself with a host of recipes that are easy and dependable yet full of flavor and pizzazz. Whether you crave the comfort of a classic meat loaf or are keen to test trendy *Vietnamese Salad Rolls with Ground Turkey*, ***125 Best Ground Meat Recipes*** will solve your dinner dilemmas. You'll be amazed at what you can accomplish, beginning with a simple pound of ground.

— **Ilana Simon**

About Ground Meat

GROUND BEEF

Generally ground beef is ground from the least tender, cheapest cuts of beef, but the grinding process tenderizes the meat and its fat content improves the flavor. Trimmings from more tender cuts may also be included.

Ground meat is made of fresh, boneless meat and has a fat content identified by one of the following terms:

Regular – maximum fat content 30 per cent
Medium – maximum fat content 23 per cent
Lean – maximum fat content 17 per cent
Extra-lean – maximum fat content 10 per cent

I used lean ground beef in all of my recipes unless otherwise stated. Lean ground beef is less dry and more economical than extra-lean, and I recommend draining excess fat whenever possible (such as when the ground beef is sautéed with onions and garlic in a skillet before combining it with other ingredients). When forming meatballs, do not overmix or press the meatballs too firmly as this toughens the ground meat when cooked.

Ground beef, which is the most popular of all ground meats, plays the starring role in numerous recipes in *125 Best Ground Meat Recipes*.

Storage Guidelines
- Store fresh ground beef in the refrigerator for no more than two days.
- Fresh ground beef can be frozen for up to four months.
- Cooked ground beef can be refrigerated for up to three days.
- Leftover cooked ground beef can be frozen for up to one month.

GROUND POULTRY

Ground poultry is made from fresh boneless, skinless chicken or turkey. Choose packages of ground poultry that are cold and tightly wrapped, without tears or holes in the plastic.

Poultry producers do not have to identify the cuts of poultry used on the ground chicken or turkey label. If cuts are identified, the product must consist solely of those specific cuts.

While the fat content of ground chicken and ground turkey packages is often not labeled, if the packaging states lean ground chicken or turkey, then the maximum fat content is 17 per cent.

I prefer cooking with the juicier ground thighs and legs (which appear darker pink in their raw state) rather than the drier ground white meat.

Due to its leanness, ground poultry, in general, is drier than ground beef and requires additional liquid when used in a casserole or meat loaf.

Ground chicken and turkey provide an excellent low-fat alternative and can replace ground beef in many dishes, if desired. They perform beautifully in barbecued burgers, saucy chilies, stews, skillets and one-dish meals.

Storage Guidelines
- Store fresh ground chicken or turkey in the refrigerator for no more than one day.
- Fresh ground chicken can be frozen for up to three months.
- Cooked ground chicken can be refrigerated for up to three days.
- Leftover cooked ground chicken can be frozen for up to one month.

GROUND PORK

Ground pork is made from fresh, boneless meat, and as with ground beef is often labeled according to the percentage of fat it contains. Lean ground pork has less than 17 per cent fat.

Ground pork should look pinkish red and fresh at the supermarket. Avoid pale meat or meat with a greenish or brownish tinge.

Ground pork excels in several Asian appetizers such as Wontons, Pot Stickers and the Caribbean-inspired Jerk Puffs.

Storage Guidelines
- Store fresh ground pork in the refrigerator for no more than two days.
- Fresh ground pork can be frozen for up to three months.
- Cooked ground pork can be refrigerated for up to three days.
- Leftover cooked ground pork can be frozen for up to one month.

GROUND LAMB

Ground lamb, often found packaged in the freezer section, is also available fresh at some supermarkets. Its fat content is not generally stated and, like other lamb cuts, it is much fattier than lean ground beef or poultry. Drain excess fat whenever possible.

Lamb has a natural full flavor and is complemented by herbs and spices. It stands out in Greek dishes, such as Lamb Moussaka and Stuffed Grape Leaves.

Lamb fat tends to congeal at room temperature, so any lamb dish you prepare should be served very hot.

Storage Guidelines
- Store fresh ground lamb in the refrigerator for no more than two days.
- Fresh ground lamb can be frozen for up to three months.
- Cooked ground lamb can be refrigerated for up to three days.
- Leftover cooked ground lamb can be frozen for up to one month.

GROUND VEAL

Ground veal is mild and lean, and its flavor is enhanced by herbs and spices, wine and tomatoes.

I love featuring veal in stews, soups and one-dish meals where its unique flavor shines through. Ground veal also marries well with ground beef in various dishes.

Storage Guidelines
- Store fresh ground veal in the refrigerator for up to two days.
- Fresh ground veal can be frozen for up to three months.
- Cooked ground veal can be refrigerated for up to three days.
- Leftover cooked ground veal can be frozen for up to one month.

SAUSAGES

Savory sausage adds a depth of flavor to pasta dishes, casseroles, stews and soups. Sausage is made from fresh, cooked or smoked ground meat. While a majority of sausages rely on ground pork as their main ingredient, today's selection includes beef, veal and poultry. The meat is usually stuffed into casings and sold in links.

Storage guidelines
- Store fresh or raw sausage in the refrigerator for up to two days.
- Store smoked sausage, such as andouille or kielbasa, in the refrigerator for up to seven days.
- Store hard sausage, such as pepperoni or jerky, in the refrigerator for up to three weeks.
- Sausage can also be frozen for up to two months.

VEGETARIAN GROUND "BEEF" REPLACEMENT

The number of vegetarian meat replacement products on the market has skyrocketed in the past few years. Crumbled ground beef replacement products are enticing vegetarians and those who want to incorporate more veggie meals into their diet to enjoy hamburger-like dishes minus the meat.

One of the bonuses of cooking with soy-based meat alternatives, which is what I used whenever ground beef replacement is called for in a recipe, is that the product is easily manipulated for different tastes and textures, ranging from Asian "meat" balls to "hamburger" soup.

Soy also provides a great low-fat source of protein. While I included a short chapter of strictly vegetarian recipes, meat alternatives can also replace ground meat in many of my other recipes.

Food Safety Tips

Proper, safe food handling and hygienic kitchen practices are key when cooking with ground meat to prevent the spread of any food-borne bacteria.

- Bacteria are found everywhere in our environment. Any meat from an animal source can harbor bacteria such as E. coli O157:H7 or salmonella. It's crucial to be extra vigilant when cooking with ground meat. If any bacteria are present on the surface of raw meat, they can end up being mixed throughout the meat during the grinding process. But through safe food handling practices, proper food storage and proper cooking methods, you can avoid any risk of food-borne illness.

- Bacteria grow rapidly when meat is stored at room temperature or what's called the danger zone: between 40°F (4°C) and 140°F (60°C). Be sure to keep hot foods hot and cold foods cold. To reduce bacteria levels, ground meat should be stored at 40°F (4°C) or colder.

- Never leave ground meat on the counter. All ground meat — beef, poultry, pork and lamb — should be thawed in the refrigerator or defrosted in the microwave, not at room temperature.

- To thaw ground meat in the refrigerator, allow 12 to 15 hours per pound (500 g).

- It is not possible to identify contaminated meat simply by looking at it or smelling it. To destroy harmful bacteria, cook ground beef, ground veal, ground lamb and ground pork to an internal temperature of 160°F (71°C). Ground chicken and turkey must be cooked to an internal temperature of 175°F (80°C).

Cooking at high temperatures kills any bacteria that may be contained within the meat. However, this measure doesn't prevent contamination of work surfaces or tools that were exposed to raw meat and poultry or their juices during storage and cooking preparation.

- Clean or disinfect counters, cutting boards and utensils with hot, soapy water after any contact with raw meat or juices.

- Store ground meat or poultry separately in the refrigerator, on its own tray or plate on the bottom shelf, to prevent cross-contamination of other ready-to-eat or prepared foods.

- If transporting ground meat in a cooler, store it in an airtight bag or container at the bottom of the cooler to prevent any drippings from contaminating other foods.

- Once you purchase ground meat, aim to refrigerate it as soon as possible on your return from the store or, better yet, pack a cooler and ice pack to safely transport it home.

- Always wash hands thoroughly in hot, soapy water before and after handling raw meat.

- Never use the same plate or tongs for cooked burgers as for raw patties.

- Wash your meat thermometer in hot, soapy water after each use.

- Leftovers should be refrigerated as soon as possible. Never let cooked ground meat sit at room temperature for more than two hours. In hot weather (86°F/30°C and higher), burgers and other ground meat dishes should not sit out for more than one hour. Remember, when in doubt, throw it out!

- Reheat all cooked ground meat casseroles, burgers and other dishes until the food is hot and steaming and registers an internal temperature of 165°F (74°C).

GROUND BEEF SAFETY

The most important means of preventing transmission of E. coli O157:H7 is to cook ground beef at a high enough temperature to kill E. coli bacteria. The only way to ensure a burger is cooked through is to use a food thermometer inserted through the side into the middle of the patty. Ground beef is safe when its internal temperature has reached 160°F (71°C).

The color on the inside of a barbecued burger (no longer pink) is not considered a reliable indicator of its doneness. Previously frozen beef burgers may turn brown in the middle before reaching a high enough temperature to kill E. coli bacteria.

Whatever cooking method you use, always ensure ground beef is cooked thoroughly by checking with a meat thermometer that the internal temperature has reached 160°F (71°C). This holds true for meat loaf, meatballs and casseroles as well as for hamburgers.

Never partially grill or cook meat for later use. Once you begin cooking, cook the ground meat completely to make certain that any bacteria are destroyed.

GROUND CHICKEN AND TURKEY SAFETY

Higher temperatures eliminate harmful organisms such as salmonella, the most common food-borne illness associated with poultry, and are critical to the control of the food-safety process.

Ground chicken and turkey burgers must always be cooked to well done or until centers are no longer pink and juices run clear.

To ensure doneness, use a good-quality, instant-read meat thermometer inserted into the middle of the patty. Ground chicken or ground turkey is cooked thoroughly once it has reached an internal temperature of 175°F (80°C). Also, when cooking meat loaves, use your meat thermometer to ensure the inside has reached this internal temperature.

Ground chicken and turkey can be defrosted in the microwave but, once thawed, should be cooked immediately. Check frequently during microwave defrosting. Remove outside portions as they thaw to prevent the edges from starting to cook before the inside thaws.

Never partially cook ground poultry for later use. Just as for ground meat, once you begin cooking, cook ground poultry completely to ensure any bacteria are destroyed.

Basic Equipment

Cooking with ground meat does not necessitate a shopping spree in the kitchenware department since most of us have on hand the appropriate utensils.

Just in case, here is a list of equipment called for throughout *125 Best Ground Meat Recipes*.

- Large 12-inch (30 cm) nonstick skillet is essential to stovetop sautéing required in many ground meat recipes.

- Electric skillet (electric fry pan) works well in many of my skillet recipes but is not mandatory (just use a large nonstick skillet with a lid in its place).

- A range of saucepans, from 10- to 12-cup (2.5 to 3 L), and a 4-quart (4 L) Dutch oven for chilies, soups and stews. I recommend stainless steel with a heavy bottom.

- Large 8-quart (8 L) stockpot for cooking pasta.

- 13-by 9-inch (3 L) ovenproof glass baking casserole dishes and 2-quart (2 L) casserole dish for one-dish meals, lasagna and other baked pasta dishes.

- Electric deep-fryer or deep wok for deep-frying appetizers such as wontons and egg rolls.

- Large baking sheets for baking appetizers and meatballs.

- Standard 9-by 5-inch (2 L) loaf pans and 12-cup muffin tins for meat loaves and mini meat loaves.

- 9-inch (23 cm) pie plates for savory pies.

Appetizers

Egg Rolls

MAKES 26 EGG ROLLS

Have you ever met anyone who didn't like egg rolls? Me neither. This recipe is perfect to double and freeze for a cocktail party or to serve as a quick nosh to your family. Spiced-up ground beef gives these egg rolls some kick. Serve hot with a variety of dipping sauces such as plum sauce, hot mustard sauce or sweet-and-sour sauce. If you don't have a deep-fryer, I offer a stovetop variation, plus baking instructions for a lower-fat option.

TIP

To fold wrappers in a rectangle: Working with 1 wrapper at a time, place on work surface with one edge facing you (square shape). (Cover remaining wrappers with a damp clean tea towel to prevent drying out.) Place 1 tbsp (15 mL) of the filling in center of egg roll wrapper. Moisten edges with beaten egg. Fold one side in, then the other side, sealing in the middle. Turn up each end and press down, forming a rectangle.

✦ Deep-fryer

4 to 6 cups	vegetable oil for deep-frying	1 to 1.5 L
1 tbsp	vegetable oil	15 mL
1	small onion, chopped	1
2	cloves garlic, minced	2
8 oz	lean ground beef	250 g
1 cup	sliced mushrooms	250 mL
½	red bell pepper, diced	½
½	green bell pepper, diced	½
1	stalk celery, chopped	1
1 tbsp	soy sauce	15 mL
2 tsp	minced fresh gingerroot	10 mL
1 tsp	chili garlic sauce	5 mL
3 cups	bean sprouts	750 mL
1	package (1 lb/500 g) egg roll wrappers (about 26)	1
1	egg, beaten	1

1. Heat oil in deep-fryer until temperature registers 375°F (190°C).

2. In a nonstick skillet, heat 1 tbsp (15 mL) oil over medium heat. Sauté onion and garlic for 3 minutes or until softened.

3. Add ground beef, mushrooms, red and green peppers, celery, soy sauce, ginger and chili garlic sauce. Sauté for 7 minutes or until ground beef is no longer pink.

4. Add bean sprouts and stir well. Sauté for 2 minutes longer. Set aside.

VARIATIONS

Stovetop: Heat 1 to 2 inches (2.5 to 5 cm) oil in a deep saucepan or wok (about 1 cup/250 mL oil) instead of a deep-fryer until temperature reaches 375°F (190°C). Use a thermometer to determine oil temperature or drop a cube of bread into the oil: if bubbles sizzle all around the bread cube, the oil is hot enough; if the temperature is too low, it will cause the food to absorb the oil and result in an overly greasy egg roll.

Baking: Another lower-fat option is to bake your egg rolls. Grease a baking sheet with vegetable spray. Place egg rolls on baking sheet and brush each lightly with vegetable oil. Bake in 375°F (190°C) oven for 25 to 30 minutes, turning once.

Use ground pork or a combination of ground pork and beef instead of only ground beef.

5. Working with 1 wrapper at a time, place on work surface with one point facing you (diamond shape). (Cover remaining wrappers with a clean damp tea towel to prevent drying out.) Spoon 1 heaping tablespoon (15 mL) of the filling on the bottom half of the wrapper, leaving a 1-inch (2.5 cm) border along the edges. Brush edges with beaten egg. Fold up the bottom corner to cover the filling. Fold in the sides and roll as for spring rolls. Brush beaten egg over seam and press firmly to seal (see Tip, far left, for folding into a rectangle).

6. Cook egg rolls, 4 at a time, in preheated deep-fryer for 2 minutes per side. Flip with tongs. Temperature should remain at about 375°F (190°C) for optimal deep-frying. Drain on paper towel.

MAKE AHEAD

Prepare filling in advance. Reheat just before assembling egg rolls. Prepare egg rolls, including deep-frying. Let cool and freeze in a single layer on baking sheets. Once frozen, transfer to airtight containers and freeze for up to 1 month. Thaw in refrigerator for a minimum of 8 hours. To reheat, bring to room temperature and place on baking sheets. Bake in 350°F (180°C) oven for 20 minutes or until heated through.

Meat Samosas

**MAKES ABOUT
24 SAMOSAS**

*This spicy meat-filled
packet is like a deep-fried
Indian ravioli. My samosas
boast an assertive curry
flavor. Samosas are
fabulous served with
mango chutney. In a pinch,
pull out the plum sauce
for a fusion pairing.*

TIP
Garam masala is an
Indian spice blend that
can be found in the
imported section or spice
section of many grocery
stores or Asian markets.

✦ Deep-fryer

4 to 6 cups	vegetable oil for deep-frying	1 to 1.5 L
1 tbsp	vegetable oil	15 mL
1	onion, chopped	1
4	cloves garlic, minced	4
1 tbsp	minced fresh gingerroot	15 mL
1 tbsp	curry powder	15 mL
1 lb	lean ground beef	500 g
1/2 tsp	salt	2 mL
1/4 tsp	freshly ground black pepper	1 mL
1 cup	frozen peas	250 mL
1 tbsp	freshly squeezed lemon juice	15 mL
1/2 tsp	hot pepper flakes	2 mL
1/2 tsp	ground cumin	2 mL
2 tbsp	chopped fresh cilantro	25 mL
1/2 tsp	garam masala (see Tip, left)	2 mL
1	package (1 lb/500 g) egg roll wrappers (about 26)	1
1	egg, beaten	1

1. Heat oil in deep-fryer until temperature registers 375°F (190°C).

2. In a nonstick skillet, heat 1 tbsp (15 mL) oil over medium-high heat. Sauté onion, garlic and ginger for 2 minutes. Add curry powder and cook, stirring continuously, for 1 minute.

3. Add ground beef, salt and pepper. Brown, breaking up meat, for 5 minutes or until no longer pink. Stir in frozen peas, lemon juice, hot pepper flakes and cumin.

4. Reduce heat to medium and cook for 1 to 2 minutes longer or until peas are softened. Drain fat from skillet. Stir in cilantro and garam masala.

5. Working with 1 egg roll wrapper at a time, brush beaten egg with a pastry brush along outside edges of wrapper. (Cover remaining wrappers with a clean damp tea towel to prevent drying out.) Spoon about 2 tbsp (25 mL) of the filling onto the center of each wrapper. Fold one corner over filling to meet opposite corner, forming a triangle. Repeat with remaining wrappers and filling.

6. Cook samosas, 3 at a time, in preheated deep-fryer for 1½ to 2 minutes per side or until golden brown. Drain on paper towel. Serve hot.

MAKE AHEAD

Prepare filling in advance. Let cool, cover and refrigerate for up to 1 day. Cooked samosas can be frozen in a single layer on a baking sheet. Once frozen, transfer to airtight container and freeze for up to 1 month. To reheat, bake in 350°F (180°C) oven for about 20 minutes or until heated through.

Crispy Wonton Bites

**MAKES 48
WONTON BITES**

These charming appetizers are a cinch to whip up, make a dramatic presentation and are palate pleasing, too. Serve warm for best results.

TIP
Greek spiced pork sausage gives "bite" to these crispy nibbles. If you can't find this kind, use another piquant variety.

VARIATION
Add 3 tbsp (45 mL) chopped oil-packed sun-dried tomatoes to sausage and feta mixture.

✦ Preheat oven to 350°F (180°C)
✦ 2 12-cup muffin tins, lightly sprayed
✦ 2 baking sheets

1 lb	Greek sausage, casings removed (see Tip, left)	500 g
1	package (1 lb/500 g) wonton wrappers (about 48)	1
	Olive oil for brushing	
1½ cups	crumbled feta cheese	375 mL
2	green onions, finely minced	2
½	red bell pepper, finely minced	½
½ cup	sliced black olives	125 mL
3 tbsp	olive oil	45 mL
3 tbsp	white wine vinegar	45 mL
1 tsp	dried oregano leaves	5 mL
½ tsp	garlic powder	2 mL
	Freshly ground black pepper, to taste	

1. In a medium skillet over medium heat, cook sausage meat, breaking up meat, for 7 minutes or until no longer pink.

2. Meanwhile, press 1 wonton wrapper into each muffin cup. Lightly brush with olive oil. Bake for 5 to 7 minutes or until golden brown. Remove wonton cups from muffin tins and place on baking sheets. Set aside. Repeat with another 24 wonton wrappers.

3. In a large bowl, combine cooked sausage meat, feta cheese, green onions, red pepper and olives. Mix well.

4. In a small bowl, whisk together olive oil, white wine vinegar, oregano, garlic powder and pepper. Pour dressing over sausage and cheese mixture. Mix well.

5. Spoon about 1 tbsp (15 mL) of the sausage mixture into each wonton cup. Bake in preheated oven for 5 to 6 minutes or until heated through.

MAKE AHEAD
Prepare filling up to 1 day in advance. Cover and refrigerate. Bake wrappers and filled cups just before serving.

Pot Stickers

Stuffed, steamed dumplings served in Japanese restaurants are called gyoza. They work well as an appetizer for any Asian-themed dinner. Serve with chili garlic sauce, sweet soy sauce, hot mustard or plum sauce.

TIPS

Round wrappers can be found at Asian food stores, often in the freezer section. Or cut wonton wrappers with a round cookie cutter.

The remaining wrappers will keep in the refrigerator for up to 1 week.

VARIATION

Use ground beef in place of ground pork.

+ Preheat oven to 250°F (120°C)
+ Large skillet with lid or electric fry pan

1 lb	lean ground pork	500 g
2 tbsp	oyster sauce	25 mL
2 tbsp	soy sauce	25 mL
2	green onions, finely chopped	2
2	cloves garlic, minced	2
2 tsp	minced fresh gingerroot	10 mL
1 tsp	sesame oil	5 mL
1/4 tsp	hot pepper flakes	1 mL
1/4 tsp	salt	1 mL
1/8 tsp	freshly ground black pepper	0.5 mL
1 lb	round (3-inch/7.5 cm) dumpling wrappers, about 68 (see Tips, left)	500 g
1/4 cup	vegetable oil, divided	50 mL
1 cup	hot chicken stock, divided	250 mL

1. In a large bowl, combine ground pork, oyster sauce, soy sauce, green onions, garlic, ginger, sesame oil, hot pepper flakes, salt and pepper. With clean hands, mix well.

2. Separate 12 dumpling wrappers on work surface and moisten top edge of each. Spoon slightly rounded teaspoon (5 mL) of the filling onto the center of each wrapper. Fold bottom half up, forming a half moon. Pinch the edges with moistened fingers to seal. Continue until first 12 pot stickers are completed.

3. In nonstick skillet or electric fry pan, heat 1 tbsp (15 mL) of the oil over medium-high heat. Fry pot stickers for about 2 minutes or until golden brown. Flip pot stickers. Add 1/4 cup (50 mL) of the hot chicken stock. Cover skillet and steam pot stickers for 2 to 2 1/2 minutes or until liquid disappears.

4. Place pot stickers on baking sheet and keep warm in preheated oven, adding batches to pan as they are ready.

5. Continue with remaining pot stickers, 12 at a time, until completed.

MAKE AHEAD

Prepare pot stickers (including frying and steaming). Let cool, then freeze in a single layer on baking sheets. To reheat, bring to room temperature and bake in 350°F (180°C) oven for 20 minutes.

Sausage Rolls

**MAKES 24
SAUSAGE ROLLS**

Nothing says "prairie party" like a pan of sausage rolls. Never mind the store-bought variety. Once you taste the homemade version, you'll be won over. The rich, buttery dough provides an excellent contrast to the salty, spicy sausage.

TIP
Serve with cold beer.

VARIATION
Use skinless farmer's sausage or another favorite sausage for this recipe. If using a thinner sausage, decrease the size of the rectangle in both height and width.

✦ Preheat oven to 425°F (220°C)
✦ Baking sheet

1 lb	bratwurst sausages	500 g
DOUGH		
2 cups	all-purpose flour	500 mL
1/4 tsp	salt	1 mL
1/3 cup	cold butter, cubed	75 mL
1/3 cup	cold shortening, cubed	75 mL
1/4 cup	cold water	50 mL

1. In a nonstick skillet over medium heat, cook sausages for 7 minutes, turning occasionally, or until browned on all sides. Slice into 1$\frac{1}{2}$-inch (4 cm) chunks. Set aside.

2. *Dough:* In a large bowl, combine flour and salt. With pastry blender or two knives, cut in butter and shortening until mixture resembles coarse crumbs.

3. Add cold water, 1 tbsp (15 mL) at a time, mixing dough with a fork until water is mixed through.

4. Roll out dough on lightly floured surface. Cut into 24 4-by 3-inch (10 by 7.5 cm) rectangles. Place 1 chunk cooked sausage onto center of each square. Fold in sides, one at a time, pinching seam. Pinch in ends and place, seam side down, on baking sheet, about 1 inch (2.5 cm) apart. Bake in preheated oven for 10 to 12 minutes or until golden brown.

MAKE AHEAD
Cook sausages as in Step 1. Slice into chunks. Prepare dough and refrigerate until required, up to 1 day in advance.

Scotch Eggs

SERVES 6

This traditional Scottish dish is best described as unusual but scrumptious. The combination of sausage and hard-cooked eggs reminds my kids of English muffin breakfast sandwiches offered at many fast-food restaurants. Scotch eggs are typically eaten cold, but I prefer them right from the oven.

TIP
Serve with HP Sauce.

VARIATIONS
Traditionally, Scotch eggs are deep-fried. Deep-fry Scotch eggs in oil heated to 375°F (190°C) for 4 to 7 minutes, turning once, until golden brown.

If desired, use bread crumbs in place of corn flakes crumbs.

✦ Preheat oven to 375°F (190°C)
✦ Broiler pan with rack

6	eggs	6
1 lb	pork sausage meat	500 g
1½ tbsp	Worcestershire sauce	22 mL
1	egg, lightly beaten	1
2 cups	corn flakes crumbs	500 mL

1. In a medium saucepan, boil eggs for 10 to 12 minutes or until hard-cooked. Pour out boiling water. Add cold water to saucepan and let eggs cool for 5 minutes. Shell and set aside.

2. In a medium bowl, combine sausage meat and Worcestershire sauce. (If using sausage links, remove sausage meat from casing.) Mix well. Divide sausage meat into 6 portions. Flatten each portion into a large, thin patty.

3. Wrap 1 patty around each hard-cooked egg, pressing seams together and sealing in each egg, ensuring there are no cracks in the meat outer layer.

4. Dip each meat-wrapped egg into beaten egg, then roll in corn flakes crumbs, patting crumbs gently into place. Place eggs on rack of broiler pan, to allow fat to drip through.

5. Bake in preheated oven for 30 to 35 minutes, turning after 15 minutes, until sausage is crisp and golden brown.

MAKE AHEAD
Prepare Scotch eggs up to 2 days in advance. Cover and refrigerate. Serve cold.

Stuffed Grape Leaves

**MAKES ABOUT 60
GRAPE LEAVES**

*Here's a party recipe that
is simply irresistible to
lovers of Greek food.
Stuffing and rolling grape
leaves is time-consuming,
but if you invite some
friends over to lend a
hand, you will savor the
experience as much as
the end results.*

TIP
Grape leaves in brine
are sold at specialty
food stores.

VARIATION
Use ground beef in
place of ground lamb.

✦ 2 large skillets

1	jar (16 oz/500 g) brine-packed grape leaves (see Tip, left)	500 g
1 tbsp	olive oil	15 mL
1	onion, chopped	1
4	cloves garlic, minced	4
1 lb	ground lamb	500 g
	Salt and freshly ground black pepper, to taste	
1 tbsp	dried oregano leaves, divided	15 mL
1 cup	cooked white long-grain rice (¼ cup/50 mL uncooked rice)	250 mL
	Zest and juice of 2 large lemons	
⅔ cup	chopped fresh dill	150 mL
½ cup	chopped fresh parsley	125 mL
1 to 2 cups	chicken stock	250 to 500 mL

1. Remove stacks of grape leaves from jar and place in boiling water for 2 minutes. Drain in colander and let cool.

2. In a large skillet, heat oil over medium heat. Sauté onion and garlic for 2 minutes. Add ground lamb and cook, breaking up meat, for 7 minutes or until no longer pink. Drain excess fat. Season with salt and pepper and half of the oregano.

3. Place cooked rice in a large bowl. Add lemon zest, all but ¼ cup (50 mL) of the lemon juice, dill, parsley and remaining oregano. Mix well. Stir in lamb mixture. Taste and adjust seasoning if necessary.

4. Set 20 grape leaves aside. Place remaining leaves, vein side up, on work surface. Spoon about 1 tbsp (15 mL) of the filling onto center of each leaf. Fold up bottom (near stem end) over filling and fold in sides. Roll up jelly roll style and set aside.

5. Line two large skillets with some of reserved loose grape leaves. Place stuffed grape leaves, seam side down, on top. Add another layer of loose grape leaves and continue stacking stuffed grape leaves on top.

6. Pour $\frac{1}{2}$ cup (125 mL) of the chicken stock and half of the remaining lemon juice over stuffed grape leaves in one skillet. Add more chicken stock, if necessary, to cover all the leaves. Repeat with second skillet.

7. Bring stock to a boil. Reduce to simmer. Place heavy plate over top of grape leaves (it should just fit inside the skillet) to weigh down the bundles while they cook. Simmer for 1 hour or until grape leaves are softened. Check occasionally and add more stock if necessary to keep moist. Remove stuffed grape leaves with tongs and let cool. Serve at room temperature.

MAKE AHEAD
Prepare filling (including rice) up to 1 day in advance.

Thai Salad with Ground Turkey

SERVES 4

This great salad does double duty as an appetizer or main-course salad. Regulate the zing factor to your liking by increasing or decreasing the hot pepper flakes.

4 oz	rice stick noodles	125 g
1 tbsp	vegetable oil	15 mL
1 lb	lean ground turkey	500 g
1	green onion, chopped	1
1	clove garlic, minced	1
SAUCE		
¼ cup	freshly squeezed lime juice	50 mL
2 tbsp	granulated sugar	25 mL
2 tbsp	soy sauce	25 mL
2 tsp	fish sauce (optional)	10 mL
½ tsp	hot pepper flakes	2 mL
1	clove garlic, minced	1
SALAD		
5 cups	romaine lettuce	1.25 L
2 cups	bean sprouts	500 mL
½	red bell pepper, thinly sliced	½
¼ cup	chopped fresh cilantro	50 mL
¼ cup	purple onion, chopped (optional)	50 mL
2 tbsp	roasted peanuts	25 mL

1. Pour boiling water over noodles or soak according to package directions. Let stand for 10 minutes. Drain.

2. In a nonstick skillet, heat oil over medium heat. Sauté ground turkey with green onion and garlic, breaking up turkey, for 7 minutes or until no longer pink. Set aside.

3. *Sauce:* Combine lime juice, sugar, soy sauce, fish sauce, if using, hot pepper flakes and garlic.

4. *Salad:* In a large salad bowl, combine rice noodles, romaine lettuce, bean sprouts and red pepper. Add ground turkey mixture. Pour sauce over top of greens and turkey and mix well. Refrigerate for at least 1 hour or for up to 6 hours to allow flavors to blend.

5. Sprinkle with cilantro, purple onion, if using, and peanuts. Serve immediately.

MAKE AHEAD
This salad can be prepared earlier in the day up to the end of Step 3. Add cilantro, purple onion, if using, and peanuts just before serving.

Wontons

MAKES 48 WONTONS

This deep-fried Chinese food favorite goes over well with both adults and children. Allow yourself about two hours to prepare and deep-fry. These freeze well.

TIPS

Chili garlic sauce is available in the Asian section of major supermarkets.

Wonton wrappers are usually found near the deli or produce sections in supermarkets.

VARIATIONS

Stovetop: Heat 1 to 2 inches (2.5 to 5 cm) oil in a deep saucepan or wok (about 1 cup/250 mL oil) instead of a deep-fryer until temperature reaches 375°F (190°C). Use a thermometer to determine oil temperature or drop a cube of bread into the oil: if bubbles sizzle all around the bread cube, the oil is hot enough; if the temperature is too low, it will cause the food to absorb oil.

Use ground beef or ground chicken in place of ground pork.

Use ¼ tsp (1 mL) hot pepper flakes in place of chili garlic sauce.

✦ Preheat oven to 250°F (120°C)
✦ Deep-fryer

4 to 6 cups	vegetable oil for deep-frying	1 to 1.5 L
8 oz	lean ground pork	250 g
2	cloves garlic, minced	2
1	green onion, minced	1
1 tbsp	minced fresh gingerroot	15 mL
1 tbsp	soy sauce	15 mL
1½ tsp	sesame oil	7 mL
1 tsp	oyster sauce	5 mL
1 tsp	chili garlic sauce (see Tips, left)	5 mL
1	package (1 lb/500 g) wonton wrappers (about 48)	1
1	egg, beaten	1
	Plum sauce	

1. Heat oil in deep-fryer until temperature registers 375°F (190°C).

2. In a large bowl, combine ground pork, garlic, green onion, ginger, soy sauce, sesame oil, oyster sauce and chili garlic sauce. Mix well.

3. Spread out 12 wonton wrappers on work surface. Spoon 1 tsp (5 mL) of the filling onto center of each.

4. Moisten outside edges of wonton wrapper with beaten egg. Fold each corner to corner to make a triangle. Bring in bottom corners (each brushed with egg wash), overlapping one on the other.

5. Cook wontons, about 8 at a time, in preheated deep-fryer for about 3 minutes or until crisp, turning after 2 minutes. Drain on paper towel. Keep warm in preheated oven. Serve warm with plum sauce.

MAKE AHEAD

Prepare wontons in advance (including deep-frying). Let cool and freeze in a single layer on baking sheets. Once frozen, transfer to airtight container and freeze for up to 1 month. Thaw in refrigerator. To reheat, bring to room temperature and bake in 350°F (180°C) oven for about 20 minutes or until heated through.

Sun-Dried Tomato and Parmesan Muffins

MAKES 20 MUFFINS

This easy appetizer is simple to prepare and tastes great. You can make these ahead and reheat when company arrives.

VARIATIONS

Omit the sun-dried tomatoes. Season filling with ½ tsp (2 mL) each dried basil and oregano.

Use shredded processed cheese block, such as Velveeta, in place of Parmesan.

+ Preheat oven to 375°F (190°C)
+ 2 12-cup muffin tins

1 tbsp	olive oil	15 mL
½	small red onion, finely minced	½
2	cloves garlic, minced	2
1 cup	diced mushrooms	250 mL
½	red bell pepper, diced	½
½	green bell pepper, diced	½
12 oz	lean ground beef	375 g
1 tsp	dried oregano leaves	5 mL
	Salt and freshly ground black pepper, to taste	
3 tbsp	chopped drained oil-packed sun-dried tomatoes	45 mL
2	packages (each 12 oz/340 g) refrigerated biscuit dough	2
½ cup	freshly grated Parmesan cheese	125 mL

1. In a skillet, heat oil over medium heat. Sauté onion, garlic, mushrooms and red and green peppers for 2 minutes.

2. Add ground beef and brown, breaking up meat, for 7 minutes or until no longer pink. Season with oregano, salt and pepper. Add sun-dried tomatoes and stir well until blended.

3. Divide biscuit dough into 20 disks. Roll out each into a 6-inch (15 cm) circle. Place 1 circle in palm of hand or on work surface. Spoon 1 tbsp (15 mL) of the filling onto dough. Top with 1 tsp (5 mL) of the Parmesan cheese. Bring up edges of dough to enclose filling, pinching in seams. Place, seam side up, in muffin cup. Repeat with remaining dough circles, filling and cheese. Bake in preheated oven for 15 minutes or until golden brown.

Crispy Wonton Bites (page 24)

Taco Salad

SERVES 4

This suppertime salad is a family favorite for a quick meal on soccer night.

TIPS
If you prefer more dressing, use approximately ½ cup (125 mL) each salsa and ranch dressing.

Serve with sour cream and guacamole.

VARIATION
Omit the tortilla chips. Serve in pre-made bowl-shaped taco shells.

1 tsp	olive oil	5 mL
1 lb	lean ground beef	500 g
¾ cup	water	175 mL
2 tbsp	Taco Seasoning Mix (see recipe, page 101)	25 mL
1	head romaine lettuce, torn into bite-size pieces	1
3	green onions, sliced	3
1	large tomato, diced	1
1 cup	shredded Cheddar cheese	250 mL
⅓ cup	sliced black olives	75 mL
⅓ cup	medium salsa	75 mL
¼ cup	ranch dressing	50 mL
1	bag (4 oz/115 g) spicy tortilla chips, broken into bite-size pieces	1

1. In a skillet, heat oil over medium heat. Brown ground beef, breaking up meat, for 7 minutes or until no longer pink. Drain excess fat.

2. Add water and taco seasoning. Mix. Reduce heat to medium-low and simmer for 10 minutes or until flavors are blended and mixture is thickened.

3. In a large bowl, combine ground beef with lettuce, green onions, tomato, cheese and black olives.

4. In a small bowl, stir together salsa and ranch dressing. Pour over taco salad and mix well. Add tortilla chips. Toss salad.

MAKE AHEAD
Prepare ground meat and salad up to 6 hours in advance, refrigerating each in separate containers. Just prior to serving, add salsa, ranch dressing and tortilla chips.

Curried Meatball Soup (page 46)

Jerk Puffs

MAKES 18 PUFFS

Spicy jerk seasoning is a Caribbean specialty usually used on grilled chicken and pork. Like Indian curries, jerk rub ingredients can vary. Likewise, jerk rubs also range in heat intensity. Watch out for this fiery rendition, adjusting the hot pepper flakes and cayenne according to preference.

TIP
Parchment paper prevents the puffs from burning on the bottom and makes for a fluffier puff.

VARIATION
Use ground beef or ground chicken in place of ground pork.

✦ Preheat oven to 400°F (200°C)
✦ Baking sheets, lined with parchment paper

1 tsp	dried onion flakes	5 mL
1 tsp	dried thyme leaves	5 mL
½ tsp	hot pepper flakes	2 mL
½ tsp	cayenne pepper	2 mL
¼ tsp	ground allspice	1 mL
¼ tsp	garlic powder	1 mL
¼ tsp	ground cinnamon	1 mL
¼ tsp	ground ginger	1 mL
¼ tsp	freshly ground black pepper	1 mL
⅛ tsp	salt	0.5 mL
1 tbsp	vegetable oil	15 mL
1	onion, chopped	1
2	cloves garlic, minced	2
1 lb	lean ground pork	500 g
1	box (14 oz/397 g) puff pastry	1
1	egg, beaten	1

1. In a small bowl, combine dried onion flakes, dried thyme leaves, hot pepper flakes, cayenne pepper, allspice, garlic powder, cinnamon, ginger, black pepper and salt. Set aside.

2. In a nonstick skillet, heat oil over medium heat. Sauté onion and garlic for 3 minutes or until onion is softened. Stir in spice mixture, mixing until combined. Add ground pork and cook, breaking up meat, for 7 minutes or until no longer pink.

3. Divide pastry in half. On a lightly floured surface, roll out each piece of puff pastry into 12-inch (30 cm) square about $\frac{1}{8}$ inch (0.3 cm) thick. Cut each into 9 4-inch (10 cm) squares.

4. Spoon about 2 tbsp (25 mL) of the filling onto center of each square. Fold into a triangle. Pinch edges together.

5. Place on prepared baking sheets, about 2 inches (5 cm) apart. Brush tops with egg. Bake in preheated oven for about 20 minutes or until golden brown.

MAKE AHEAD
Prepare up to the end of Step 4 and refrigerate, covered, for up to 1 day in advance. Or freeze on baking sheets. Once frozen, transfer to resealable bag and freeze for up to 1 month.

Perishky

This Mennonite specialty is labor-intensive, but the filled rolls make excellent appetizers or kids' lunches. Thanks to recipe tester Cheryl Warkentin for supplying the wonderful yeast dough used in this recipe.

TIP

If you don't have leftover mashed potatoes on hand, simply cook 1 to 2 potatoes in the microwave, then peel off skin and mash as usual.

VARIATION

Use a combination of ground beef and ground pork instead of only ground beef.

✦ Preheat oven to 350°F (180°C)
✦ 2 baking sheets

DOUGH

3 cups	all-purpose flour	750 mL
½ cup	granulated sugar	125 mL
1 tbsp	quick-rise (instant) yeast	15 mL
1½ tsp	salt	7 mL
1 cup	scalded milk, cooled	250 mL
½ cup	cold water	125 mL
⅓ cup	vegetable oil	75 mL

FILLING

1 tbsp	vegetable oil	15 mL
1	onion, chopped	1
1	clove garlic, minced	1
8 oz	lean ground beef	250 g
1 cup	mashed potatoes	250 mL
2 tbsp	chopped fresh dill	25 mL
½ tsp	salt	2 mL
	Freshly ground black pepper, to taste	

1. *Dough:* In a large bowl, combine flour, sugar, yeast and salt. Make a well in the center. Pour in milk, water and oil. Mix and knead to form a soft dough. Cover and let rise until doubled in size, about 1 hour.

2. *Filling:* In a skillet, heat oil over medium heat. Sauté onion for 2 minutes. Add garlic and sauté for 1 minute longer or until softened.

3. Add ground beef and brown, breaking up meat, for 7 minutes or until no longer pink. Add mashed potatoes, dill, salt and pepper. Reduce heat to low and simmer, stirring occasionally, for 5 minutes to allow flavors to blend.

4. Roll out dough to ¼-inch (0.5 cm) thickness. Cut into 4-by 3-inch (10 by 7.5 cm) rectangles. Spoon 1½ tbsp (22 mL) of the filling onto center of each rectangle. Bring long sides together, then pinch each end to form rectangular pillows.

5. Place, seam side down with ends tucked under, about 2 inches (5 cm) apart on baking sheets. Cover and let rise for about 30 minutes or until puffed. Bake in preheated oven for 15 to 20 minutes or until lightly browned. Serve hot.

MAKE AHEAD

Prepare filling up to 1 day in advance. Cooked perishky will keep for up to 3 days in the refrigerator. Or freeze in a single layer on a baking sheet. Once frozen, transfer to airtight container and freeze for up to 1 month. To reheat, bake in 350°F (180°C) oven for 20 minutes or until warmed through.

Vietnamese Salad Rolls with Ground Turkey

MAKES 32 SALAD ROLLS

Salad rolls are one of my favorite Vietnamese dishes, so I devised a recipe that incorporates easy-to-prepare ground turkey along with salad roll staples such as fresh mint leaves and bean sprouts. I hope you enjoy these as much as I do for a light lunch or appetizer.

TIPS

Rice wrappers and rice stick noodles are available at Asian markets and in some grocery stores.

To rehydrate rice stick noodles, soak in hot water for 10 minutes or according to package directions until tender. Drain.

For a neater look, fold in the sides of the wrap before rolling.

VARIATION

Use ground chicken or pork in place of ground turkey.

◆ Wok

1 tbsp	vegetable oil	15 mL
2	green onions, chopped	2
2	cloves garlic, minced	2
1 lb	lean ground turkey	500 g
¼ cup	hoisin sauce	50 mL
2 tbsp	creamy or smooth peanut butter	25 mL
1 tbsp	freshly squeezed lime juice	15 mL
1 tbsp	soy sauce	15 mL
32	6-inch (15 cm) rice wrappers (see Tips, left)	32
¼ cup	fresh mint leaves	50 mL
2 cups	rehydrated rice stick noodles or cooked vermicelli, drained (see Tips, left)	500 mL
2 cups	bean sprouts	500 mL
1	English cucumber, peeled and sliced thinly into 2-inch (5 cm) long sticks	1

DIPPING SAUCE

½ cup	hoisin sauce	125 mL
2 to 3 tbsp	chopped salted peanuts	25 to 45 mL

1. In a wok or large skillet, heat oil over medium-high heat. Sauté green onions and garlic for 1 minute.

2. Add ground turkey and cook, breaking up turkey, for 7 minutes or until no longer pink.

3. In a small bowl, combine hoisin sauce, peanut butter, lime juice and soy sauce. Mix well. Pour over ground turkey mixture, stirring well until combined. Transfer to a bowl. Let cool.

4. Meanwhile, soak 1 rice wrapper at a time in a shallow bowl of warm water for about 45 seconds or until softened. Transfer to a clean tea towel and pat dry on both sides. Place wrapper on work surface. Place 3 mint leaves along center of each rice wrapper. Spoon about 1 tbsp (15 mL) of the ground turkey mixture over mint leaves. Top with 1 tbsp (15 mL) each noodles and bean sprouts, then 2 cucumber sticks. Fold bottom of rice wrapper up, then fold in one side and roll, leaving the top open. Place salad roll, seam side down, on serving platter. Cover loosely with a damp towel and plastic wrap. Continue with remaining rice wrappers and filling. Serve at room temperature.

5. *Dipping Sauce*: In a small bowl, combine hoisin sauce and peanuts. Serve with salad rolls for dipping.

MAKE AHEAD

Salad rolls can be prepared up to 1 day in advance. Cover with a damp towel and wrap in plastic and refrigerate. Bring to room temperature before serving.

Chicken and Wild Mushroom Bundles

MAKES 60 BUNDLES

This attractive appetizer will impress your guests and leave you beaming from the compliments. Despite the lengthy instructions, once you get the hang of creating the bundles, they're a breeze.

✦ Preheat oven to 350°F (180°C)
✦ 2 large baking sheets

2 tbsp	butter	25 mL
1	small onion, minced	1
3	cloves garlic, minced	3
2 cups	chopped mixed mushrooms, such as shiitake, oyster and button	500 mL
8 oz	lean ground chicken	250 g
1 tbsp	all-purpose flour	15 mL
1/2 cup	half-and-half (10%) cream	125 mL
2 tbsp	chopped fresh parsley	25 mL
1 tsp	freshly squeezed lemon juice	5 mL
1/2 tsp	dried thyme leaves	2 mL
1/2 tsp	salt	2 mL
	Freshly ground black pepper, to taste	
6	sheets phyllo pastry, thawed	6
1/2 cup	butter, melted	125 mL

1. In a nonstick skillet, melt 2 tbsp (25 mL) butter over medium heat. Sauté onion and garlic for 3 minutes or until softened.

2. Add mushrooms and sauté for 3 minutes longer. Add ground chicken and cook, breaking up chicken, for 7 minutes or until no longer pink.

3. Sprinkle flour over chicken and mushrooms. Stir until blended. Gradually add cream, stirring, until mixture comes to a boil over medium heat.

4. Remove from heat. Stir in parsley, lemon juice, thyme, salt and pepper.

5. Unfold phyllo and place 1 sheet on a clean work surface. Top with second sheet to form a double layer. (Cover remaining phyllo sheets with a clean damp tea towel to prevent drying out.) Brush pastry with melted butter.

6. Using a pizza cutter or sharp knife, cut phyllo into 20 3-inch (7.5) squares. Spoon about 1 tsp (5 mL) of the mushroom and chicken mixture onto center of each square. Gather up corners of phyllo and pinch just above filling, twisting to seal. Brush outsides of bundles lightly with melted butter. Continue with remaining phyllo pastry and filling. Place on baking sheets.

7. Bake in preheated oven for 10 to 12 minutes or until pastry is golden.

MAKE AHEAD
Bundles can be prepared up to the end of Step 6. Freeze unbaked bundles in a single layer on a baking sheet. Once frozen, transfer to airtight container and freeze for up to 1 month. Bake bundles directly from freezer in preheated 350°F (180°C) oven for 25 to 30 minutes or until heated through and golden brown.

Curried Chicken Tartlets

MAKES 24 SMALL TARTLETS

Puff pastry makes for elegant shells and a simple, stylish appetizer.

TIP

You will have some excess dough left over. For a more meat pie like tartlet, roll out remaining dough and cut out smaller circles to place on top of filling. Seal edges closed.

✦ Preheat oven to 400°F (200°C)
✦ 2 mini-muffin tins (12 cups each)

1 tsp	vegetable oil (approx.)	5 mL
1 lb	lean ground chicken	500 g
½	onion, minced	½
2	cloves garlic, minced	2
½ cup	sliced mushrooms	125 mL
2 tbsp	prepared mustard	25 mL
2 tbsp	liquid honey	25 mL
1½ tbsp	curry powder	22 mL
⅓ cup	chicken stock (approx.)	75 mL
2 tbsp	currants (optional)	25 mL
1	box (14 oz/397 g) puff pastry	1
1	egg, beaten	1

1. In a nonstick skillet, heat oil over medium heat. Cook ground chicken, breaking up chicken, for 7 minutes or until no longer pink. Remove from pan with slotted spoon and set aside.

2. In same nonstick skillet, sauté onion, garlic and mushrooms for 3 to 5 minutes or until browned, adding more oil if necessary.

3. In a bowl, mix together mustard, honey and curry powder. Pour over onions, stirring until combined.

4. Return chicken to skillet. Pour in chicken stock, stirring until chicken is well coated with curry sauce. Simmer for 15 minutes or until thickened, adding more chicken stock if necessary to prevent sticking. Stir in currants, if using.

5. Divide puff pastry in half. On a lightly floured surface, roll out each half to 12-inch (30 cm) square about $\frac{1}{8}$ inch (0.3 cm) thick. Cut each sheet into 12 3-inch (7.5 cm) circles.

6. Place 1 circle in a muffin cup, molding dough up the side to form a tartlet shell. Spoon 1 to 2 tbsp (15 to 25 mL) of the curried chicken filling onto center of each shell. Repeat with remaining puff pastry circles and filling. Bake in preheated oven for 8 to 10 minutes or until tartlets are golden brown.

MAKE AHEAD

Prepare filling up to 1 day in advance. Refrigerate baked tartlets for up to 2 days. To reheat, warm in 350°F (180°C) oven for 20 minutes or until cooked through. Freeze baked tartlets on baking sheets. Once frozen, transfer to resealable bag and freeze for up to 1 month.

Chopped Liver

MAKES ABOUT 3 CUPS
(750 ML)

A Jewish deli delicacy gets a makeover. The chicken schmaltz of traditional chopped liver is recreated by browning the onions until crisp and adding a packet of chicken bouillon.

TIP

Chopped liver is great served on challah (egg bread) as an appetizer. Slice bread into little squares and top with a dollop of chopped liver for a delectable nibble. It is similar to pâté or mousse sold in gourmet food shops.

VARIATION

My dad Monte Simon's father, Alex (my grandfather), opened the famous Winnipeg landmark Simon's Delicatessen. Accordingly, my dad knows a little about chopped liver and recommends additional oil and salt to make my lighter-hearted version more like traditional deli chopped liver. Add up to ¼ cup (50 mL) more oil when sautéing onions and season generously with salt. Also, don't be afraid to use an extra-large onion, and if you can find it, use beef liver.

* Preheat oven 375°F (190°C)
* Baking sheet

1½ lbs	chicken livers	750 g
¼ cup	vegetable oil, divided	50 mL
1	large onion, chopped	1
1	packet chicken bouillon powder (about 1 tbsp/15 mL)	1
2	hard-cooked eggs, peeled and quartered	2
	Salt and freshly ground black pepper, to taste	

1. Place chicken livers on baking sheet. Bake in preheated oven for 25 to 30 minutes, turning once, or until just a hint of pink remains. (Do not overbake the livers or they will become tough.) Let cool for 10 minutes.

2. Meanwhile, in a skillet, heat 2 tbsp (25 mL) of the oil over medium-low heat. Sauté onions for 15 minutes or until starting to brown. Increase heat to medium, add remaining oil and sauté for 10 minutes longer or until onions are crisp.

3. Sprinkle chicken bouillon over onions, stirring until combined.

4. In a food processor, combine cooked liver, fried onions and hard-cooked eggs. Season generously with salt and pepper. Process with on/off pulses just until minced. Do not overprocess.

MAKE AHEAD

Chopped liver can be prepared in advance. Refrigerate in a covered container for up to 3 days.

Soups

Curried Meatball Soup

If you're crazy about curry, you'll love this soup. Simmering the meatballs directly in the broth gives it great depth of flavor. The vermicelli also adds a welcome texture.

TIP

This makes a thick soup. If desired, add 2 cups (500 mL) more stock.

VARIATIONS

Use homemade chicken stock or 2 cans (each 10 oz/284 mL) condensed chicken broth prepared according to directions.

Use spaghetti in place of thinner vermicelli.

5 cups	chicken stock	1.25 L
2¼ tsp	curry powder, divided	11 mL
1	small onion, chopped	1
2	stalks celery, chopped	2
1	carrot, chopped	1
½ cup	cauliflower florets	125 mL
8 oz	lean ground beef	250 g
¼ tsp	salt	1 mL
¼ tsp	garlic powder	1 mL
⅛ tsp	freshly ground black pepper	0.5 mL
1 tbsp	mango chutney	15 mL
4 oz	vermicelli, broken up (about 1½ cups/375 mL)	125 g

1. In a Dutch oven or large saucepan over medium-high heat, combine chicken stock and 2 tsp (10 mL) of the curry powder. Bring to a boil.

2. Add onion, celery, carrot and cauliflower. Boil for 3 minutes.

3. Meanwhile, season ground beef with salt, garlic powder, pepper and remaining curry powder. Stir in mango chutney. Mix well. Form into 12 ¾-inch (2 cm) meatballs.

4. Add meatballs to saucepan. Reduce heat to medium-low and simmer, covered, for 25 minutes or until meatballs are no longer pink.

5. Add vermicelli. Increase heat to medium-high and bring to a boil. Reduce heat to low and simmer for 12 minutes or until pasta is cooked.

Italian Wedding Soup

SERVES 6 TO 8 AS AN APPETIZER OR 4 TO 6 AS A MAIN COURSE

This attractive meatball soup is often served as an appetizer at — you guessed it — Italian weddings. Its combination of spinach, basil, ground veal and ground beef makes for a super flavor-packed zuppa!

TIP

Serve with fresh sourdough bread on a cold winter's night and your family won't even know you've snuck some healthy spinach into their meal.

VARIATIONS

Use all ground veal.

Add an additional 1 cup (250 mL) spinach for extra vitamins.

✦ Preheat oven to 350°F (180°C)
✦ Baking sheet, lightly sprayed

8 oz	lean ground veal	250 g
8 oz	lean ground beef	250 g
1/4 cup	dry bread crumbs	50 mL
1 1/2 tbsp	chopped fresh parsley	22 mL
1/2 tsp	dried Italian seasoning	2 mL
1	egg, beaten	1
8 cups	chicken stock	2 L
2 cups	chopped fresh spinach	500 mL
1/2 cup	alphabet or other small pasta	125 mL
1 tbsp	chopped fresh basil	15 mL

1. In a medium bowl, combine ground veal, ground beef, bread crumbs, parsley, Italian seasoning and egg. Form into 24 1-inch (2.5 cm) meatballs. Place on prepared baking sheet. Bake in preheated oven for 25 to 30 minutes, turning after 15 minutes, or until well browned on all sides and no longer pink.

2. In a large saucepan over medium-high heat, bring chicken stock to a boil. Add spinach, alphabet pasta and basil. Cover and boil for 5 minutes.

3. Add meatballs to broth. Reduce heat to low and simmer, uncovered, for 3 minutes or until pasta is completely cooked.

MAKE AHEAD

Refrigerate cooked meatballs for up to 2 days. Or freeze in a single layer on baking sheet. Once frozen, transfer to resealable bag and freeze for up to 1 month. If prepared in advance, reheat in 350°F (180°C) oven for about 20 minutes or until heated through before adding to soup pot.

Pasta e Fagioli Soup

SERVES 6 TO 8 AS AN APPETIZER OR 4 TO 6 AS A MAIN COURSE

This is another great meal in a bowl, with the added bonus of a large helping of fiber thanks to the beans. The fresh basil adds a special flavor that cannot be duplicated by its dried counterpart in this recipe.

TIPS

I prefer to cook the pasta separately because when cooked directly in the soup, this amount of pasta would absorb too much water and release so much starch that it would alter the intended consistency of this already thick soup. Smaller amounts of pasta can often be cooked directly in the soup.

The soup freezes well in an airtight container. If intending to freeze, omit the carrots and do not add the pasta.

VARIATION

Use chickpeas (garbanzo beans) in place of navy beans.

1 tbsp	olive oil	15 mL
1 cup	chopped onion	250 mL
3	cloves garlic, minced	3
2	stalks celery, chopped	2
2	carrots, peeled and sliced	2
1 lb	lean ground beef	500 g
5 cups	beef stock	1.25 L
3 cups	tomato-based vegetable cocktail	750 mL
1	can (28 oz/796 mL) diced tomatoes, including juice	1
1	can (19 oz/540 mL) red kidney beans, drained and rinsed	1
1	can (19 oz/540 mL) white navy beans, drained and rinsed	1
6 tbsp	chopped fresh basil	90 mL
1/2 tsp	salt	2 mL
	Freshly ground black pepper, to taste	
1/4 tsp	hot pepper flakes	1 mL
1 1/2 cups	small pasta shells	375 mL
	Freshly grated Parmesan cheese	

1. In a Dutch oven or large saucepan, heat oil over medium heat. Sauté onion, garlic, celery and carrots for 3 minutes or until softened.

2. Add ground beef and brown, breaking up meat, for 7 minutes or until no longer pink.

3. Add beef stock, vegetable cocktail, diced tomatoes with juice, kidney beans, navy beans, basil, salt, pepper and hot pepper flakes. Increase heat to medium-high and bring to a boil. Reduce heat to low and simmer, uncovered, for about 1 hour or until thickened. Stir occasionally, breaking up tomatoes.

4. Meanwhile, in a large pot of boiling salted water, cook pasta shells for 8 minutes or until al dente. Drain. Add to saucepan. Stir well and simmer for 5 minutes longer.

5. Ladle soup into bowls. Top each serving with Parmesan cheese.

MAKE AHEAD

If serving the same day, slice onion, garlic and carrots in advance.

Quick Ground Veal and Chickpea Soup

SERVES 8 AS AN APPETIZER OR 4 AS A MAIN COURSE

The chickpeas blend well with the veal and mushrooms and create a hearty winter soup. Using fresh herbs takes this speedy soup up a notch.

TIP

If using store-bought chicken stock, season with salt sparingly since canned and boxed chicken stock are very salty.

VARIATIONS

Use other small pasta in place of alphabets.

Use 2 tsp (10 mL) each dried basil and dill seed in place of fresh herbs.

1 tbsp	olive oil	15 mL
1 cup	chopped onion	250 mL
4	cloves garlic, minced	4
1 lb	lean ground veal	500 g
	Salt and freshly ground black pepper, to taste	
8 cups	chicken stock (see Tip, left)	2 L
2	carrots, peeled and sliced	2
2	zucchini, sliced	2
1	can (19 oz/540 mL) chickpeas (garbanzo beans), drained and rinsed	1
1 cup	alphabet pasta	250 mL
1	can (10 oz/284 mL) whole mushrooms, drained	1
2 tbsp	chopped fresh basil	25 mL
2 tbsp	chopped fresh dill	25 mL

1. In a Dutch oven or large saucepan, heat oil over medium heat. Sauté onion and garlic for 3 minutes or until onions are softened.

2. Add ground veal and brown, breaking up meat, for 7 minutes or until no longer pink. Season with salt and pepper.

3. Add chicken stock, carrots, zucchini and chickpeas. Increase heat to medium-high and bring to a boil. Reduce heat to medium-low and simmer, uncovered, for 15 minutes or until vegetables are almost softened.

4. Add pasta, mushrooms, basil and dill. Simmer, covered, for 15 minutes or until pasta is tender.

Veal and Wild Mushroom Soup

SERVES 4 TO 6

On a cold winter's day, this hearty soup warms the soul. Despite the lengthy list of ingredients and instructions, it is easy enough to make for your family and has just the right amount of elegance for serving to company.

TIP
Herbes de Provence is a flavorful blend of herbs, usually rosemary, marjoram, thyme, savory, basil, lavender and sage.

VARIATION
Use other small pasta such orecchiette, which is a rice-shaped pasta.

1	package (1/2 oz/14 g) dried wild mushrooms	1
1 tbsp	olive oil	15 mL
2	shallots, minced	2
2	cloves garlic, minced	2
1 cup	sliced wild mushroom mixture, such as shiitake and oyster	250 mL
1 lb	lean ground veal	500 g
1/2 tsp	dried thyme leaves	2 mL
	Salt and freshly ground black pepper, to taste	
3/4 cup	dry red wine, divided	175 mL
5 cups	beef stock	1.25 L
2	carrots, peeled and sliced	2
2	stalks celery, sliced	2
1 tsp	herbes de Provence (see Tip, left)	5 mL
1	can (19 oz/540 mL) romano beans, drained and rinsed	1
1/2 cup	orzo pasta	125 mL
1/4 cup	chopped fresh parsley (approx.)	50 mL

1. In a heatproof bowl, pour 1 cup (250 mL) boiling water over dried mushrooms. Let stand for 15 minutes, then strain through a sieve, reserving liquid. Chop mushrooms.

2. In a nonstick skillet, heat oil over medium heat. Sauté shallots and garlic for 3 minutes or until softened.

3. Reduce heat to low. Add fresh mushrooms and sauté for 8 minutes or until mushrooms start to sweat.

4. Add ground veal and rehydrated dried wild mushrooms and brown, breaking up meat, for 7 minutes or until no longer pink. Season with thyme, salt and pepper.

5. Gradually pour in $\frac{1}{2}$ cup (125 mL) of the red wine and reserved mushroom soaking liquid. Increase heat to medium-high and bring to a boil. Reduce heat to medium-low and simmer for 10 minutes.

6. Meanwhile, in a Dutch oven or large saucepan over medium-high heat, bring stock and remaining red wine to a boil. Add carrots, celery and herbes de Provence. Boil, covered, for 5 minutes.

7. Stir in veal mixture, beans and orzo. Boil, covered, for 4 minutes. Add parsley and boil for 4 minutes longer or until orzo is tender. Serve topped with additional parsley.

Ground Chicken and Wild Mushroom Soup

*Earthy exotic mushrooms
give this soup an intense
flavor. Portobello and
shiitake mushrooms,
once thought of as wild,
are now cultivated and
readily available in your
neighborhood supermarket.*

TIP
This delicious soup
makes a great meal
in a bowl. Serve with
crusty fresh bread.

VARIATION
Use cremini (brown)
mushrooms in place of
button mushrooms. Use
other wild mushrooms,
such as oyster, or a
combination of oyster,
shiitake and portobello.

1 tbsp	butter	15 mL
½ cup	chopped onion	125 mL
2	cloves garlic, minced	2
4 cups	chopped wild mushroom mixture, such as portobello and shiitake	1 L
1 cup	chopped button mushrooms	250 mL
¼ tsp	dried thyme leaves	1 mL
	Salt and freshly ground black pepper, to taste	
1 tbsp	olive oil	15 mL
1 lb	lean ground chicken	500 g
2	carrots, peeled and sliced	2
2	stalks celery, sliced	2
8 cups	chicken stock	2 L
½ cup	pot barley	125 mL
2	large sprigs fresh dill, chopped	2

1. In a Dutch oven or large saucepan, heat butter over medium-low heat. Sauté onion for 3 minutes. Add garlic and wild and button mushrooms and sauté for 8 minutes or until mushrooms begin to sweat. Season with thyme, salt and pepper.

2. Meanwhile, in nonstick skillet, heat oil over medium heat. Brown ground chicken, breaking up chicken, for 7 minutes or until no longer pink. Season with salt and pepper. Add carrots and celery and sauté for 4 minutes longer.

3. Add ground chicken mixture to mushroom mixture. Pour in stock and barley. Add dill. Increase heat to medium-high and bring to a boil. Reduce heat to low and simmer, uncovered, for 1 hour or until barley is tender.

MAKE AHEAD
Slice onions, carrots and celery and mince garlic. Place in separate bowls and refrigerate for up to 8 hours in advance.

Smoked Sausage and Lentil Soup

SERVES 4 TO 6

Smoky sausage and lentils marry well in this satisfying soup. Incorporating more fiber-friendly pulses into your family's diet is not always easy, but this soup is so scrumptious that they won't even notice it's healthy, too! I use lower-fat smoked turkey sausage as well.

TIP
If the broth is too thick, add an additional 1 cup (250 mL) chicken stock.

VARIATIONS
Use another variety of smoked sausage such as kielbasa or garlic smoked sausage.

Use green lentils in place of brown lentils, but check soup after 30 minutes since they take less time to cook.

1 tbsp	olive oil	15 mL
1	onion, chopped	1
2	cloves garlic, minced	2
8 oz	smoked turkey sausage, sliced into rounds	250 g
2	carrots, peeled and sliced	2
2	stalks celery, chopped	2
1	parsnip, peeled and sliced	1
5 cups	chicken stock	1.25 L
1½ cups	small brown lentils	375 mL
¼ cup	chopped fresh parsley	50 mL
1½ tsp	herbes de Provence (see Tip, page 50)	7 mL
	Freshly ground black pepper, to taste	

1. In a Dutch oven or large saucepan, heat oil over medium heat. Sauté onion for 2 minutes. Add garlic and sauté for 1 minute.

2. Add sausage slices and cook, turning to brown on all sides, for 5 minutes. Add carrots, celery and parsnips. Sauté for 5 minutes longer.

3. Pour in stock. Add lentils, parsley, herbes de Provence and pepper. Increase heat to medium-high and bring to a boil. Reduce heat to medium-low and simmer, covered, for 40 minutes or until lentils are tender.

MAKE AHEAD

Like most soups, this rendition improves with age. Make 1 to 2 days in advance of serving or freeze. If planning to freeze, omit carrots and parsnips, which become mushy once frozen. Freeze in airtight container for up to 1 month.

Smoky Mexican Bean Soup

*This is a great soup to
serve to a large crowd. I
throw in the cauliflower
to give it more body. It
pairs nicely with the
smoked chicken and
turkey sausage.*

VARIATIONS
Use white beans in
place of black beans.

Substitute your favorite
smoked sausage.

1	can (28 oz/796 mL) crushed tomatoes	1
5 cups	chicken stock	1.25 L
2 tbsp	tomato paste	25 mL
1 tbsp	minced canned chipotle chilies in adobo sauce	15 mL
½ tsp	dried thyme leaves	2 mL
½ tsp	cumin seeds	2 mL
½ tsp	dried oregano leaves	2 mL
1 tbsp	olive oil	15 mL
1	onion, chopped	1
2	cloves garlic, minced	2
1 lb	smoked chicken or turkey sausage, sliced into 1-inch (2.5 cm) chunks	500 g
1	can (19 oz/540 mL) black beans, drained and rinsed	1
1	can (12 oz/341 mL) corn kernels	1
½	cauliflower head, cut into florets	½
¼ cup	chopped fresh cilantro	50 mL

1. In a Dutch oven or large saucepan over medium-high heat, bring crushed tomatoes, chicken stock, tomato paste, chipotle chilies, thyme, cumin seeds and oregano to a boil. Reduce heat to low and simmer, covered, for 30 minutes or until thickened.

2. Meanwhile, in a large nonstick skillet, heat oil over medium heat. Sauté onion and garlic for 3 minutes or until onion is softened. Add sausage chunks and sauté for 7 minutes, turning frequently, until browned on all sides.

3. Add sausage mixture to broth. Add black beans, corn kernels, cauliflower florets and cilantro. Increase heat to medium-high and bring to a boil. Reduce heat to medium-low and simmer, uncovered, for 15 minutes or until cauliflower is tender.

MAKE AHEAD
This soup can be prepared in advance and refrigerated for up to 2 days or frozen until required. If freezing, do not add cauliflower florets. Instead, once soup has thawed, steam cauliflower in microwave for 5 minutes on High and add to pot before reheating.

Creamy Wild Rice and Chicken Soup

SERVES 8 AS AN APPETIZER OR 4 TO 6 AS A MAIN COURSE

Fall is the perfect time to indulge in wild rice. The gourmet grain (actually an aquatic grass, not rice) is harvested in late August in swampy areas, chiefly in Manitoba, Saskatchewan, Ontario, Alberta and Minnesota. Wild rice is the only cereal native to Canada and is found primarily in shallow water along river and stream shores, and occasionally at lake sites featuring a slow and constant water current.

TIP

I microwave rather than boil the wild rice. To microwave, rinse ½ cup (125 mL) wild rice and combine with 2 cups (500 mL) hot water in a covered 8-cup (2 L) microwave-safe glass casserole. Microwave on High for 5 minutes. Microwave on Medium for 30 minutes longer. Add more water if necessary and microwave for 5 to 10 minutes longer or until water is absorbed and rice is fully cooked, light gray in color, split and curled. Let stand for 15 minutes, then rinse and drain.

⅓ cup	butter	75 mL
½ cup	all-purpose flour	125 mL
5 cups	chicken stock, divided	1.25 L
1 tbsp	butter	15 mL
1	small onion, chopped	1
2	cloves garlic, minced	2
½ cup	sliced mushrooms	125 mL
1	stalk celery, sliced	1
½ cup	dry white wine	125 mL
2 cups	cooked wild rice (½ cup/125 mL uncooked) (see Tip, left)	500 mL
8 oz	lean ground chicken	250 g
1 tsp	vegetable oil (optional)	5 mL
1 cup	half-and-half (10%) cream or milk	250 mL
	Salt and freshly ground pepper, to taste	

1. In a Dutch oven or large saucepan, melt ⅓ cup (75 mL) butter over medium heat. Whisk in flour and cook for 1 minute longer.

2. Gradually whisk in 3 cups (750 mL) of the chicken stock, stirring until smooth.

3. Bring to boil over medium heat, stirring constantly. Add remaining broth. Reduce heat to low and simmer, covered, for 10 minutes or until thickened.

4. Meanwhile, in a skillet, melt 1 tbsp (15 mL) butter over medium heat. Sauté onion, garlic, mushrooms and celery for 5 minutes or until softened. Reduce heat to low. Stir in wine and cook for 3 minutes. Transfer to thickened broth along with cooked wild rice.

5. Add ground chicken to same skillet adding 1 tsp (5 mL) oil if necessary to prevent sticking. Brown, breaking up chicken, for 7 minutes or until no longer pink. Transfer to broth. Stir in cream. Season with salt and pepper. Simmer, covered, for 20 minutes, stirring occasionally, until flavors are blended and heated through.

Wonton Soup

MAKES 48 WONTONS

Ground turkey makes for a lighter wonton than the usual pork filling. If desired, you can use the traditional ground pork, but you'll be pleasantly surprised at how wonderful boiled turkey wontons are in this scrumptious soup. The recipe serves four, but I use a whole package of wontons. Serve them with the soup for sure, but they're also good on their own or you can freeze some for later (see Make Ahead, far right).

TIP
Be sure not to overstuff wontons or the wrappers will split open. If desired, after forming triangle, fold in bottom corners, sealing one on top of the other. Boil as directed.

VARIATION
Use ground chicken or ground beef in place of ground turkey.

WONTONS

1 lb	lean ground turkey	500 g
1/2 cup	chopped fresh mushrooms	125 mL
4	green onions, minced	4
2	cloves garlic, minced	2
2 tbsp	tamari or soy sauce	25 mL
2 tsp	sesame oil	10 mL
1/8 tsp	salt	0.5 mL
1/8 tsp	freshly ground black pepper	0.5 mL
1 tbsp	cornstarch	15 mL
1	package (1 lb/454 g) wonton wrappers	1

SOUP

5 cups	chicken stock	1.25 L
1 cup	chopped fresh spinach	250 mL
1/2 cup	broccoli florets	125 mL
1	carrot, peeled and sliced	1
1 tbsp	tamari or soy sauce	15 mL

1. *Wontons:* In a bowl, combine turkey, mushrooms, green onions, garlic, tamari, sesame oil, salt and pepper. Sprinkle with cornstarch.

2. Fill a medium saucepan with water and bring to a boil. Lay wonton wrappers on work surface. Spoon 2 tsp (10 mL) of the filling onto center of each wrapper. Brush water around outside edges. Fold corner to corner to form a triangle. Seal.

3. Cook wontons, 8 at a time, in boiling water for 4 minutes or until they float to the top. Drain in colander. Repeat until all wontons are cooked or freeze a portion (see Make Ahead, right).

4. *Soup:* In a large saucepan over medium-high heat, bring chicken stock to a boil. Add spinach, broccoli, carrot and tamari. Boil for 3 minutes. Add 12 to 16 wontons and boil for 1 minute longer or until heated through. Ladle soup into 4 bowls and serve steaming hot.

MAKE AHEAD

Wontons are ideal for making ahead and freezing. Freeze uncooked in a single layer on a baking sheet. Once frozen, transfer to a resealable bag and freeze for up to 1 month. Do not thaw before boiling. Add directly to boiling water and cook for 6 to 8 minutes or until they float to the top.

Hamburger Soup

What would a ground meat cookbook be without a hearty hamburger soup recipe? As with most soups, you can throw in any extra vegetables you may have on hand. Serve with crusty bread for dinner in a bowl.

TIP

If the soup is too thick, add an additional ½ to 1 cup (125 to 250 mL) water.

1 lb	lean ground beef	500 g
1	stalk celery, chopped	1
1	large carrot, peeled and sliced	1
1	onion, chopped	1
1	clove garlic, minced	1
1 tsp	vegetable oil	5 mL
1	can (28 oz/796 mL) diced tomatoes, including juice	1
1	can (14 oz/398 mL) red kidney beans, drained and rinsed	1
1	can (10 oz/284 mL) condensed tomato soup, undiluted	1
½ cup	sliced mushrooms	125 mL
2 tsp	Worcestershire sauce	10 mL
Pinch	cayenne pepper	Pinch
	Salt and freshly ground black pepper, to taste	
1	zucchini, chopped	1
2 tbsp	chopped fresh parsley	25 mL
	Freshly grated Parmesan cheese (optional)	

1. In a nonstick skillet over medium heat, brown ground beef, breaking up meat, for 7 minutes or until no longer pink. With slotted spoon, transfer to a Dutch oven or large saucepan.

2. In same nonstick skillet, sauté celery, carrot, onion and garlic for 5 minutes or until softened. (Add a small amount of oil if necessary to prevent sticking.) Add to saucepan.

3. Add diced tomatoes, kidney beans, tomato soup, 1 can (10 oz/284 mL) water, mushrooms, Worcestershire sauce, cayenne pepper, salt and pepper. Increase heat to medium-high and bring to a boil. Reduce heat to low and simmer, uncovered and stirring occasionally, for 30 minutes or until thickened and tomatoes have broken down.

4. Add zucchini and parsley and simmer for 15 minutes longer or until zucchini is tender. Serve with Parmesan cheese, if desired.

MAKE AHEAD

This soup freezes well but if you intend to do so, omit the carrots. Freeze in airtight container for up to 1 month.

Chilies & Stews

Chipotle Beef Chili

Chipotle chilies add a fiery, smoky flavor to this chili, making it a stand-out from your run-of-the-mill chili. If you like it really hot, increase the chipotle chilies. Serve over cooked rice, if you like, with additional cilantro and tortilla chips on the side.

VARIATIONS

If you're a big fan of cilantro, increase to ½ cup (125 mL) chopped fresh cilantro.

If canned chipotles are unavailable, use the same amount of chipotle-flavored barbecue sauce instead.

1 tbsp	olive oil	15 mL
1	onion, chopped	1
2	cloves garlic, minced	2
1 lb	lean ground beef	500 g
1	can (28 oz/796 mL) diced tomatoes, including juice	1
1½ tbsp	minced canned chipotle chilies in adobo sauce (see Tips, right)	22 mL
1	can (14 oz/398 mL) red kidney beans, drained and rinsed	1
1 cup	frozen corn kernels	250 mL
1 tbsp	chili powder (see Tips, pages 62 and 64)	15 mL
1 tsp	ground cumin	5 mL
¼ cup	chopped fresh cilantro	50 mL
2 tbsp	freshly squeezed lime juice	25 mL

1. In a saucepan, heat oil over medium heat. Sauté onion and garlic for 3 minutes or until onion is softened.

2. Add ground beef and brown, breaking up meat, for 7 minutes or until no longer pink.

Chipotle chilies are smoked, dried jalapeño peppers and are often canned in a tomato adobo sauce. Look for them at specialty Latin American stores and gourmet food shops.

Purée the whole can of chipotle chilies in adobo sauce with a hand blender or regular blender. Store in a container in the refrigerator or freeze in ice cube trays and then place cubes in a resealable bag for easy use. One ice cube compartment holds about 1 to 2 tbsp (15 to 25 mL) liquid. Since ice cube trays come in different sizes, check the size of the ice cube tray first before freezing the puréed chipotle chilies so you know exactly the amount in each cube. This makes it simple to measure the required amounts and includes both the sauce and the pepper.

3. Stir in diced tomatoes with juice, chipotle chilies, kidney beans, corn kernels, chili powder and cumin. Increase heat to medium-high and bring to a boil. Reduce heat to low and simmer, stirring occasionally, for 1 hour or until thickened. Taste partway through cooking and adjust seasoning. Add more chipotle chilies, if desired.

4. In the last 15 minutes of cooking, stir in cilantro and lime juice.

MAKE AHEAD

This chili can be prepared in advance up to the end of Step 3 and refrigerated for up to 2 days or frozen for up to 1 month. During reheating, stir in fresh cilantro and lime juice.

Can't Miss Chili

SERVES 6

My husband, Ari Marantz, is famous for the spicy chili he's been making since his university ski trip days. This is it.

TIPS

Chili powder is sold in varying degrees of spiciness. If your chili powder is mild, you may want to add an additional 1 to 2 tbsp (15 to 25 mL) for a more intense flavor.

For a great combination, serve chili over cooked white rice and top with shredded Cheddar cheese.

2 tbsp	vegetable oil	25 mL
1/2	large onion, chopped	1/2
1	large clove garlic, minced	1
1	large jalapeño pepper, seeded and chopped	1
1	large green bell pepper, chopped	1
1/2	large red bell pepper, chopped	1/2
1 1/2 lbs	lean ground beef	750 g
1/2 tsp	salt	2 mL
1/4 tsp	freshly ground black pepper	1 mL
1	can (28 oz/796 mL) whole tomatoes, including juice	1
2	cans (each 14 oz/398 mL) red kidney beans, drained and rinsed	2
3 tbsp	chili powder (see Tips, left and page 64)	45 mL
1/4 tsp	cumin seeds	1 mL

1. In a large saucepan, heat oil over medium-high heat. Sauté onion, garlic and jalapeño for 3 minutes or until onion is golden brown.

2. Add green and red peppers, ground beef, salt and pepper. Increase heat to high and brown, breaking up meat, for 5 minutes or until no longer pink.

3. Remove saucepan from heat and drain off excess fat. Reduce heat to medium and return saucepan to stovetop. Add tomatoes with juice and crush while stirring with a large spoon. Add kidney beans, chili powder and cumin seeds. Mix well.

4. Increase heat to medium-high and bring to a boil. Reduce heat to low and simmer, uncovered or with a splatter screen over saucepan, stirring often, for 1 hour or until thickened.

MAKE AHEAD

This is the perfect make-ahead dish: it improves with age and can easily be reheated in the microwave. Store chili in a microwave-safe dish in the refrigerator for up to 3 days or freeze in an airtight container for up to 1 month. Thaw before reheating. Reheat in a microwave-safe dish on High, stirring partway through, for 20 minutes or until heated through.

Coney Island Sauce

MAKES ABOUT 2½ CUPS (625 ML) SAUCE, ENOUGH FOR 4 TO 6 HAMBURGERS

This thin chili sauce is ideal for serving on hot dogs or burgers. Who needs to go out for fast food when you can throw some hamburgers on the grill and recreate this topping at home?

TIPS

If you prefer a more sour sauce, add 2 tbsp (25 mL) white vinegar after 20 minutes. Cook for 5 minutes longer.

This recipe can easily be doubled.

VARIATIONS

For a hotter sauce, add additional cayenne.

1 tsp	vegetable oil	5 mL
8 oz	lean ground beef	250 g
2	cloves garlic, minced	2
1	can (5½ oz/156 mL) tomato paste	1
1 cup	water	250 mL
2 tbsp	sweet relish	25 mL
1 tbsp	chili powder (see Tips, pages 62 and 64)	15 mL
1 tsp	Worcestershire sauce	5 mL
1 tsp	steak sauce (such as HP Sauce)	5 mL
½ tsp	salt	2 mL
¼ tsp	freshly ground black pepper	1 mL
⅛ tsp	cayenne pepper	0.5 mL
⅛ tsp	paprika	0.5 mL

1. In a saucepan, heat oil over medium heat. Sauté ground beef and garlic for 7 minutes or until beef is no longer pink.

2. Add tomato paste, water, relish, chili powder, Worcestershire sauce, steak sauce, salt, black pepper, cayenne pepper and paprika. Increase heat to medium-high and bring to a boil.

3. Reduce heat to low and simmer for 20 minutes, stirring occasionally, until bubbling and thickened.

MAKE AHEAD

This recipe is ideal for making ahead to serve at an evening barbecue. Refrigerate in covered container for up to 3 days.

Greasy Spoon Chili

If you fancy the kind of chili you'd be served at a lunch counter or greasy spoon, this is it. It's thin in texture and rich in flavor. The secret ingredient is coffee! It's great served on its own, but you could also try it over French fries or potato skins or on burgers or hot dogs.

TIP

Make sure your chili powder is fresh. If you've stored it longer than 6 months, it has likely lost some of its zip. In that case, add ½ tsp (2 mL) hot pepper flakes or cayenne pepper for more heat.

VARIATION

For a thicker, more traditional chili, add 1 can (19 oz/540 mL) red kidney beans, drained and rinsed, when you add the green pepper and celery.

1 tsp	vegetable oil	5 mL
1 lb	lean ground beef	500 g
1	onion, chopped	1
1	clove garlic, minced	1
1	jalapeño pepper, seeded and minced	1
1½ cups	regular brewed coffee	375 mL
1 cup	beef stock	250 mL
1	can (14 oz/398 mL) tomato sauce	1
1	can (5½ oz/156 mL) tomato paste	1
2 tbsp	chili powder (heaping) (see Tips, left and page 62)	25 mL
1 tsp	curry powder	5 mL
1 tsp	dried oregano leaves	5 mL
½ tsp	ground cumin	2 mL
½ tsp	ground coriander	2 mL
1	stalk celery, chopped	1
½	green bell pepper, chopped	½
1 tsp	granulated sugar	5 mL
	Salt and freshly ground black pepper, to taste	

1. In a Dutch oven or large saucepan, heat oil over medium heat. Brown ground beef for 2 minutes. Add onion, garlic and jalapeño pepper. Sauté, breaking up meat, for about 5 minutes longer or until no longer pink. Drain off excess fat.

2. Add coffee, beef stock, tomato sauce, tomato paste, chili powder, curry powder, oregano, cumin and coriander.

3. Reduce heat to low and simmer, uncovered or with a splatter screen, stirring occasionally, for 1 hour or until flavors are blended.

4. Add celery, green pepper, sugar, salt and pepper. Simmer for 30 minutes longer or until thickened.

MAKE AHEAD

This chili can be made in advance and frozen in an airtight container for up to 1 month. Thaw before reheating. Reheat in microwave-safe dish on High, stirring partway through, for 20 minutes or until heated through.

Chipotle Beef Chili (page 60)

Turkey and Black Bean Chili

SERVES 4

Turkey and black beans make a great pairing in this Southwest-inspired creation.

VARIATIONS
Use red hot pepper sauce in place of the green version — but less of it since it is much hotter.

Serve chili topped with shredded Monterey Jack cheese.

1 tbsp	olive oil	15 mL
1	onion, finely chopped	1
2	cloves garlic, minced	2
1	jalapeño pepper, seeded and minced	1
½	green bell pepper, chopped	½
½	red bell pepper, chopped	½
1 lb	lean ground turkey	500 g
1	can (28 oz/796 mL) diced tomatoes, including juice	1
1	can (19 oz/540 mL) black beans, drained and rinsed	1
2 tbsp	chopped fresh cilantro (approx.)	25 mL
1 tbsp	balsamic vinegar	15 mL
¾ tsp	ground cumin	4 mL
¾ tsp	ground coriander	4 mL
½ tsp	cayenne pepper	2 mL
5	drops green jalapeño hot pepper sauce	5

1. In a Dutch oven or large saucepan, heat oil over medium heat. Sauté onion for 3 minutes. Add garlic, jalapeño and green and red peppers. Sauté for 2 minutes longer or until peppers are softened.

2. Add ground turkey and brown, breaking up turkey, for 7 minutes or until no longer pink. Add tomatoes with juice, black beans, cilantro, balsamic vinegar, cumin, coriander, cayenne pepper and hot pepper sauce. Increase heat to medium-high and bring to a boil.

3. Reduce heat to low and simmer, uncovered or with splatter screen, stirring occasionally, for 45 minutes or until chili is thickened.

4. Serve sprinkled with additional fresh cilantro.

MAKE AHEAD
Prepare chili up to 3 days in advance and refrigerate. Reheat in microwave-safe dish on High, stirring partway through, for 20 minutes or until heated through.

Salsa Hamburgers (page 75)

Chocolate Chili

This spicy dish really is not meant for dessert! Chocolate gives it a rich flavor. See if anyone can guess the secret ingredient.

TIP
If you can find it, use Mexican chocolate for a more authentic dish.

VARIATION
Use ground turkey in place of ground beef.

1 tbsp	vegetable oil	15 mL
1	onion, chopped	1
2	cloves garlic, minced	2
½	green bell pepper, chopped	½
½	red bell pepper, chopped	½
1 lb	lean ground beef	500 g
1	can (28 oz/796 mL) whole tomatoes, including juice	1
1 cup	beef stock	250 mL
1	can (19 oz/540 mL) black beans, drained and rinsed	1
1	bay leaf	1
1½ tbsp	chili powder (see Tips, pages 62 and 64)	22 mL
1½ tsp	dried oregano leaves	7 mL
1 tsp	cumin seeds	5 mL
½ tsp	cayenne pepper	2 mL
½ tsp	ground cinnamon	2 mL
2 oz	bittersweet chocolate, grated	60 g

1. In a large saucepan, heat oil over medium heat. Sauté onion, garlic and green and red peppers for 3 minutes or until softened.

2. Add ground beef. Brown, breaking up meat, for 7 minutes or until no longer pink.

3. Add tomatoes with juice and crush while stirring with a large spoon. Add beef stock, black beans, bay leaf, chili powder, oregano, cumin seeds, cayenne and cinnamon.

4. Increase heat to medium-high and bring to a boil. Reduce heat to low and simmer, uncovered, stirring occasionally, for 45 minutes or until thickened.

5. Taste and adjust seasoning. For a spicier chili, add more cayenne or chili powder.

6. Stir in grated chocolate. Simmer for 20 minutes longer. Discard bay leaf before serving.

Ground Turkey Sloppy Joes

SERVES 4

This old standby gets an overhaul by replacing ground beef with trendy ground turkey and adding a splash of beer. Serve Sloppy Joes over open-faced Kaiser rolls with a green salad for a nutritious and easy child-friendly chow.

VARIATIONS

Use apple cider in place of beer.

Use ground beef in place of ground turkey.

1 tbsp	vegetable oil	15 mL
½	onion, finely chopped	½
2	cloves garlic, minced	2
½	green bell pepper, diced	½
1	stalk celery, diced	1
1 lb	lean ground turkey	500 g
	Salt and freshly ground black pepper, to taste	
1 cup	prepared chili sauce	250 mL
½ cup	beer	125 mL
½ cup	barbecue sauce	125 mL
2 tbsp	white vinegar	25 mL
4	crusty buns	4

1. In a medium saucepan, heat oil over medium heat. Sauté onion, garlic, green pepper and celery for 3 minutes or until vegetables are softened.

2. Add ground turkey. Brown, breaking up turkey, for 7 minutes or until no longer pink. Season with salt and pepper.

3. Add chili sauce, beer and barbecue sauce. Increase heat to medium-high and bring to a boil.

4. Reduce heat to low. Add vinegar. Simmer, uncovered, stirring occasionally, for 20 minutes or until thickened.

5. Slice buns in half. Spoon turkey mixture over each half and serve open-faced.

MAKE AHEAD

This recipe can easily be doubled and prepared in advance. Freeze half in an airtight container for up to 1 month. Thaw and reheat in microwave-safe dish on High, turning partway through, for 20 minutes.

Sausage and Potato Stew

SERVES 4 TO 6

*This is the perfect antidote
to the chills on a frosty
day. Serve with fresh
pumpernickel bread
for a hearty meal.*

TIP

Prepare up to 3 days
in advance and
refrigerate. Before
serving, let come to
room temperature.
Reheat in preheated
350°F (180°C) oven for
25 to 30 minutes or
until heated through.

VARIATION

Use turkey sausage or
another mild sausage
in place of chorizo.

1 lb	soft chorizo sausage	500 g
½ cup	chopped onion	125 mL
1	stalk celery, chopped	1
1 cup	chopped red bell pepper	250 mL
1 cup	chopped green bell pepper	250 mL
1	carrot, peeled and sliced	1
2	cloves garlic, minced	2
	Olive oil (optional)	
1	bottle (12 oz/341 mL) beer	1
1	can (28 oz/796 mL) stewed tomatoes, including juice	1
2	potatoes, peeled and cubed	2
1	zucchini, sliced	1
2 tsp	dried Italian seasoning	10 mL
	Chopped fresh parsley	
	Freshly grated Parmesan cheese	

1. Slice sausage into 1-inch (2.5 cm) pieces. In a Dutch oven or large saucepan over medium heat, cook sausage for 8 minutes, turning occasionally, until browned on all sides.

2. Add onion and sauté for 2 minutes. Add celery, red and green peppers, carrot and garlic. Sauté for 3 minutes longer, adding olive oil if necessary to prevent sticking.

3. Pour in beer and stewed tomatoes with juice. Add potatoes and zucchini. Season with Italian seasoning.

4. Increase heat to medium-high and bring to a boil. Reduce heat to medium-low and simmer, covered, for 15 minutes or until potatoes are tender.

5. Serve sprinkled with parsley and Parmesan cheese.

Smoked Sausage and Turkey Stew with Chipotle Chilies

SERVES 4

The robust flavors of this stew (from the sausage, roasted peppers and chipotle chilies in adobo sauce) make it a must-serve on a cold winter's day. Reminiscent of paella, this stew is best enjoyed served over rice. And try to ensure there are leftovers for a luscious next-day lunch.

TIP

To roast peppers, grill on a grill pan under broiler, turning occasionally, for 20 to 25 minutes or until blackened and blistered on all sides. Immediately place in a pot with a tight-fitting lid and let sweat for several minutes. (This will make peppers easier to peel.) Cut off stem. Peel and seed.

VARIATIONS

In place of chipotle chilies, stir in ½ jalapeño, seeded and minced, when adding sausage to saucepan. But be warned: the flavor won't be as wonderful.

Use chicken breast in place of turkey breast.

Use your favorite smoked sausage in place of the turkey sausage.

1 tbsp	olive oil	15 mL
1	onion, chopped	1
4	cloves garlic, minced	4
8 oz	smoked turkey sausage, sliced into rounds	250 g
1 lb	boneless skinless turkey breast, cut into 1-inch (2.5 cm) cubes	500 g
1	can (28 oz/796 mL) diced tomatoes, including juice	1
1	red bell pepper, roasted (see Tip, left)	1
1	green bell pepper, roasted	1
1 tsp	dried thyme leaves	5 mL
½ tsp	dried basil leaves	2 mL
¼ tsp	dried rosemary	1 mL
¼ tsp	saffron threads	1 mL
1 tbsp	chipotle chilies in adobo sauce, minced or puréed	15 mL

1. In a Dutch oven or large saucepan, heat oil over medium heat. Sauté onion for 2 minutes. Add garlic and sauté for 1 minute longer.

2. Add sausage and cook for 7 minutes, turning until browned on all sides and no longer pink.

3. Increase heat to medium-high. Add turkey breast. Sauté for 5 minutes or until no longer pink.

4. Add tomatoes with juice and roasted red and green peppers. Bring to a boil. Season with thyme, basil, rosemary and saffron. Stir in chipotle chilies in adobo sauce.

5. Reduce heat to low and simmer for 15 minutes or until thickened and flavors are combined.

Meatball and Rigatoni Stew

Facing the usual dinnertime dilemma? Don't despair. This dish offers meatballs in a new and improved format.

MEATBALLS

1 lb	lean ground beef	500 g
¼ cup	dry bread crumbs	50 mL
1 tbsp	dried onion flakes	15 mL
1 tbsp	Worcestershire sauce	15 mL
1 tsp	dry mustard	5 mL
½ tsp	salt	2 mL
¼ tsp	freshly ground black pepper	1 mL
1	egg, beaten	1

STEW

1 tbsp	olive oil	15 mL
1	onion, chopped	1
2	cloves garlic, minced	2
2	stalks celery, chopped	2
1	can (28 oz/796 mL) diced tomatoes, including juice	1
1½ tbsp	white vinegar	22 mL
1½ tsp	Worcestershire sauce	7 mL
1½ tsp	soy sauce	7 mL
1 tsp	granulated sugar	5 mL
½ tsp	chili powder	2 mL
½ tsp	dried thyme leaves	2 mL
½ tsp	dried basil leaves	2 mL
⅛ tsp	cayenne pepper	0.5 mL
	Salt and freshly ground black pepper, to taste	
1½ cups	rigatoni	375 mL
2½ cups	beef stock	625 mL
1	zucchini, sliced	1
	Freshly grated Parmesan cheese (optional)	

1. *Meatballs:* In a medium bowl, combine ground beef, bread crumbs, onion flakes, Worcestershire sauce, mustard, salt, pepper and egg. Shape into 24 1-inch (2.5 cm) meatballs.

2. In a skillet over medium heat, brown meatballs, turning once, for 8 minutes or until no longer pink. Set aside.

3. *Stew:* In a Dutch oven or large saucepan, heat oil over medium heat. Sauté onion, garlic and celery for 3 minutes or until softened.

4. Add diced tomatoes with juice, vinegar, Worcestershire sauce, soy sauce, sugar, chili powder, thyme, basil, cayenne, salt and pepper. Mix well.

5. Increase heat to medium-high and bring to a boil. Reduce heat to medium-low and simmer, uncovered, stirring occasionally, for 20 minutes or until thickened.

6. Meanwhile, in a large saucepan of boiling salted water, cook pasta for about 8 minutes or until al dente. Drain and let cool.

7. After tomato sauce has simmered for 20 minutes, add beef stock and zucchini. Return to a boil over medium heat. Stir in meatballs and pasta and boil gently for 5 minutes or until heated through. Sprinkle with Parmesan cheese, if desired.

MAKE AHEAD

This dish can be made up to 1 day in advance. Let cool, cover and refrigerate. Transfer to 12-cup (3 L) casserole. Reheat in preheated 375°F (190°C) oven for 35 to 40 minutes.

Easy Ground Beef Stew

This simple stew is fast and tasty and easy on the pocketbook. The added bonus: your family will love it.

TIP
No additional salt is added due to the inclusion of already salted ingredients such as onion soup mix and canned mushrooms.

VARIATION
Use 1 cup (250 mL) fresh sliced mushrooms and ½ cup (125 mL) water in place of canned mushrooms and liquid.

1 tbsp	vegetable oil	15 mL
1	small onion, chopped	1
2	cloves garlic, minced	2
2	stalks celery, sliced	2
1 lb	lean ground beef	500 g
4	potatoes, peeled and cubed	4
2	carrots, peeled and sliced	2
1	parsnip, peeled and sliced	1
1	can (10 oz/284 mL) mushroom stems and pieces, including liquid	1
1	pouch (1.3 oz/39 g) onion soup mix	1
1 tbsp	all-purpose flour	15 mL
¼ cup	water	50 mL

1. In a nonstick skillet, heat oil over medium heat. Sauté onion, garlic and celery for 3 minutes or until softened.

2. Add ground beef. Brown, breaking up meat, for 7 minutes or until no longer pink. Drain off excess fat.

3. Meanwhile, in a large saucepan over medium-high heat, cover potatoes, carrots and parsnips with about 4 cups (1 L) water and bring to a boil. Boil for 10 to 12 minutes or until just starting to soften.

4. Remove from heat and add mushrooms with liquid, onion soup mix and ground beef mixture. Return saucepan to medium heat. Cooked, covered, for 8 minutes longer or until vegetables are tender and flavors are blended.

5. When vegetables are tender, mix flour with water and whisk into stew until combined. Cook over medium heat, stirring continuously, for 5 minutes or until flour is blended in and stew is thickened. Serve immediately.

BBQ Burgers

Cheesy Horseradish Burgers

MAKES 6 BURGERS

The twist in these beef burgers is the addition of prepared horseradish and processed cheese. Try them topped with Coney Island Sauce (see recipe, page 63) for an excellent pairing.

TIP

These burgers are egg-free thanks to the horseradish, which provides the necessary amount of moisture.

VARIATION

Use regular Cheddar cheese in place of processed cheese block.

✦ Preheat barbecue

1 lb	lean ground beef	500 g
1/2 cup	dry bread crumbs	125 mL
2 tbsp	prepared horseradish	25 mL
1/2 tsp	salt	2 mL
1/4 tsp	freshly ground black pepper	1 mL
1/8 tsp	garlic powder	0.5 mL
4 oz	processed cheese block, such as Velveeta, thinly sliced (see Variation, left)	125 g
6	hamburger buns, split and lightly toasted	6

1. In a large bowl, combine ground beef, bread crumbs, horseradish, salt, pepper and garlic powder. Mix well. Shape into 12 $1/4$-inch (0.5 cm) thick patties. Center cheese slices over 6 of the patties, leaving at least $1/2$-inch (1 cm) border around edge. Place remaining patties on top of cheese and pinch at edges to seal.

2. Place on preheated barbecue over medium heat. Cook, turning once, for 7 to 8 minutes per side or until no longer pink.

3. Serve in toasted buns. Garnish with your favorite toppings, such as Dijon mustard, lettuce, pickles and tomatoes.

Salsa Hamburgers

MAKES 8 BURGERS

Salsa adds sizzle to your burgers and keeps them juicy. Be sure to use tortilla chip crumbs; they provide excellent flavor.

TIPS

To make tortilla chip crumbs, place chips in a blender or food processor and process until fine.

Serve with sliced avocado, purple onion and shredded lettuce.

VARIATIONS

Add additional cilantro, if desired.

Use mozzarella in place of Monterey Jack cheese.

✦ Preheat barbecue

1½ lbs	lean ground beef	750 g
½ cup	plain tortilla chip crumbs (see Tips, left)	125 ml
½ cup	medium salsa	125 mL
1 tbsp	chopped fresh cilantro	15 mL
1	clove garlic, minced	1
	Salt and freshly ground black pepper, to taste	
8	slices Monterey Jack cheese (optional)	8
8	hamburger buns, split and lightly toasted	8

1. In a large bowl, combine ground beef, tortilla chip crumbs, salsa, cilantro, garlic, salt and pepper. Mix well. Shape into 8 ½-inch (1 cm) thick patties.

2. Place on preheated barbecue over medium heat. Cook, turning once, for 7 to 8 minutes per side or until no longer pink.

3. Top each burger with 1 slice Monterey Jack cheese, if desired, just before burgers are ready. Grill for 1 minute longer or until cheese is melted.

4. Serve in toasted buns. Garnish with your favorite toppings, such as Dijon mustard, lettuce, pickles and tomatoes.

MAKE AHEAD

Prepare patties early in the day and refrigerate. Barbecue when desired.

Ranch Burgers

✦ Preheat barbecue

MAKES 4 BURGERS

Creamy ranch dressing adds to the mystique of this outstanding burger.

TIP
Do not overmix meat mixture or the meat will become tough.

VARIATIONS
Use all ground beef or all ground veal.

For a different flavor, use another favorite creamy dressing, such as creamy Caesar, in place of the peppercorn ranch dressing.

8 oz	lean ground veal	250 g
8 oz	lean ground beef	250 g
1/4 cup	dry bread crumbs	50 mL
1/4 cup	onion, finely minced	50 mL
2	cloves garlic, minced	2
1/4 tsp	salt	1 mL
1/4 tsp	freshly ground pepper	1 mL
1	egg, beaten	1
3 tbsp	peppercorn ranch dressing	45 mL
1/2 tsp	dried parsley flakes	2 mL
4	hamburger buns, split and lightly toasted	4

1. In a medium bowl, combine ground veal, ground beef, bread crumbs, onion, garlic, salt and pepper. Mix well.

2. In a small bowl, whisk together egg, peppercorn ranch dressing and parsley flakes. Stir into ground meat mixture, mixing gently until combined. Shape into 4 3/4-inch (2 cm) thick patties.

3. Place on preheated barbecue over medium heat. Cook, turning once, for about 8 minutes per side or until no longer pink.

4. Serve in toasted buns. Garnish with your favorite toppings.

Italian Veal Burgers

MAKES 4 BURGERS

Use freshly grated Parmesan cheese for best results. The pimento gives the burgers a lovely red color throughout.

TIP
Pimento is Spanish sweet red pepper often used to stuff green olives. You can use roasted red pepper in place of pimento.

VARIATION
Use half ground beef and half ground veal.

✦ Preheat barbecue

1 lb	lean ground veal	500 g
1/3 cup	freshly grated Parmesan cheese	75 mL
1/4 cup	dry bread crumbs	50 mL
1/4 cup	finely minced onion	50 mL
2	cloves garlic, minced	2
2 tbsp	pimento, chopped (see Tip, left)	25 mL
1	egg, beaten	1
1 tsp	dried Italian seasoning	5 mL
1/4 tsp	salt	1 mL
1/4 tsp	freshly ground black pepper	1 mL
4	slices fontina or mozzarella cheese	4
4	crusty Italian buns, split and lightly toasted	4

1. In a medium bowl, combine ground veal, Parmesan cheese, bread crumbs, onion, garlic, pimento, egg, Italian seasoning, salt and pepper. Mix well. Shape into 4 3/4-inch (2 cm) thick patties.

2. Place on preheated barbecue over medium heat. Cook, turning once, for about 8 minutes per side or until no longer pink.

3. Top with cheese. Serve in toasted buns.

Smoky Chicken Burgers

MAKES 4 BURGERS

Barbecuing is an excellent method for preparing lean ground chicken. The chicken stays moist thanks to the addition of hickory barbecue sauce, which also imparts a sophisticated smoky flavor.

VARIATIONS

Use ground beef instead of chicken.

For cheese chicken burgers, place thin slices of mozzarella or Swiss cheese on patties for the last minute of barbecuing.

✦ Preheat barbecue

1 lb	lean ground chicken	500 g
½ cup	dry bread crumbs	125 mL
1	egg, beaten	1
2 tbsp	freshly grated Parmesan cheese	25 mL
2 tbsp	hickory barbecue sauce	25 mL
1 tsp	dried onion flakes	5 mL
1 tsp	dried oregano leaves	5 mL
½ tsp	garlic powder	2 mL
½ tsp	salt	2 mL
¼ tsp	freshly ground black pepper	1 mL
4	whole wheat hamburger buns, split and lightly toasted	4

1. In a large bowl, combine chicken, bread crumbs, egg, Parmesan cheese, barbecue sauce, onion flakes, oregano, garlic powder, salt and pepper. Mix well. Shape into 4 ¾-inch (2 cm) thick patties.

2. Place on preheated barbecue over medium heat. Cook, turning once, for about 8 minutes per side or until no longer pink.

3. Serve in toasted buns. Garnish with your favorite toppings. Dijon mustard pairs well with chicken burgers.

Teriyaki Chicken Burgers

MAKES 6 BURGERS

Teriyaki sauce takes the everyday burger up a notch. Try this Asian-influenced burger once and you'll be hooked. Serve with fried rice and Japanese cucumber salad. I use panko crumbs — Japanese bread crumbs — instead of regular bread crumbs because they are coarser and add a nice crunchy texture to the burger.

TIPS

Panko crumbs are coarse Japanese bread crumbs. Look for them in Asian markets.

If using soy sauce, also add a pinch of ginger and a splash of sake or sherry to replicate teriyaki sauce.

Top burgers with purple onion, wasabi mayonnaise and grainy mustard.

VARIATION

Use coarse dry bread crumbs in place of panko crumbs.

◆ Preheat barbecue

1 lb	lean ground chicken	500 g
½ cup	panko crumbs (see Tips, left)	125 mL
1 tbsp	dried onion flakes	15 mL
2 tbsp	teriyaki or soy sauce (see Tips, left)	25 mL
1 tbsp	liquid honey	15 mL
2	cloves garlic, minced	2
6	hamburger buns, split and lightly toasted	6

1. In a medium bowl, combine ground chicken, panko crumbs and onion flakes.

2. In a small bowl, combine teriyaki sauce, honey and garlic cloves. Mix well. Stir into ground chicken mixture until combined. Shape into 6 ½-inch (1 cm) thick patties.

3. Place on preheated barbecue over medium heat. Cook, turning once, for 7 to 8 minutes per side or until no longer pink.

4. Serve in toasted buns. Garnish with your favorite toppings (see Tips, left).

Venison Burgers

Game for some game? Hunters' catches frequently turn up as a base for burgers in combination with ground beef. In these barbecued burgers, venison's gamey flavor comes through — but it doesn't bonk you over the head.

TIP
Game requires a longer barbecuing time. Watch carefully to avoid overcooking.

VARIATION
Use all ground beef for your everyday burger.

✦ Preheat barbecue

8 oz	ground venison	250 g
8 oz	lean ground beef	250 g
1/2 cup	dry bread crumbs	125 mL
1	egg, beaten	1
1 tbsp	hickory barbecue sauce	15 mL
1/2 tsp	garlic powder	2 mL
1/2 tsp	salt	2 mL
1/4 tsp	freshly ground black pepper	1 mL
6	hamburger buns, split and lightly toasted	6

1. In a large bowl, combine ground venison, ground beef, bread crumbs, egg, barbecue sauce, garlic powder, salt and pepper. Mix well. Shape into 6 1/2-inch (1 cm) thick patties.

2. Place on preheated barbecue over medium heat. Cook, turning once, for 10 to 12 minutes per side or until no longer pink (see Tip, left).

3. Serve in toasted buns. Garnish with your favorite toppings, such as pickles, tomatoes, onion and lettuce.

Ostrich Burgers

MAKES 6 BURGERS

Ostrich farms have popped up across North America over the past decade, meeting a growing demand for the lean poultry that looks, and tastes, more like ground beef. Look for ground ostrich at specialty food stores and farmer's markets. It is very lean, so brush the patties well with oil before grilling to prevent sticking.

VARIATION

Instead of barbecuing, sauté in olive oil in a skillet for about 16 minutes, turning several times.

✦ Preheat barbecue

1 lb	lean ground ostrich	500 g
2	cloves garlic, minced	2
1/4 cup	dry bread crumbs	50 mL
1 tbsp	dried onion flakes	15 mL
1 tbsp	Dijon mustard	15 mL
1	egg, beaten	1
1/2 tsp	dried thyme leaves	2 mL
1/2 tsp	dried tarragon leaves	2 mL
1/2 tsp	dried parsley flakes	2 mL
1/2 tsp	salt	2 mL
1/4 tsp	freshly ground black pepper	1 mL
	Vegetable oil for brushing	
6	hamburger buns, split and lightly toasted	6

1. In a medium bowl, combine ground ostrich, garlic, bread crumbs, onion flakes, mustard, egg, thyme, tarragon, parsley, salt and pepper. Mix well. Shape into 6 1/2-inch (1 cm) thick patties.

2. Brush patties with oil. Place on preheated barbecue over medium heat. Cook, turning once, for 7 to 8 minutes per side or until no longer pink.

3. Serve in toasted buns. Garnish with your favorite toppings, such as mustard, ketchup, pickles, lettuce, tomatoes and onions.

Bison Burgers

MAKES 6 BURGERS

On the Prairies, where the buffalo used to roam, bison burgers and other regional fare are showing up on the menus of the trendiest restaurants. A gastronomical grassroots movement has spread across the country, with chefs committed to buying local products. The result is a bounty of bison and other Prairie products to tempt our taste buds and our curiosity.

TIP

Bison is available at specialty and gourmet food stores. Ingredients are kept simple in this recipe so as not to detract from the gamey bison flavor.

VARIATION

Add 1 tbsp (15 mL) dried onion flakes.

◆ Preheat barbecue

1 lb	ground bison (see Tip, left)	500 g
½ tsp	minced fresh gingerroot	2 mL
1	clove garlic, minced	1
½ tsp	salt	2 mL
¼ tsp	freshly ground black pepper	1 mL
6	hamburger buns, split and lightly toasted	6

1. In a large bowl, combine ground bison, ginger, garlic, salt and pepper. Mix well. Shape into 6 ½-inch (1 cm) thick patties.

2. Place on preheated barbecue over medium heat. Cook, turning once, for 7 to 8 minutes per side or until no longer pink.

3. Serve in toasted buns. Garnish with your favorite toppings, such as mustard, lettuce, pickles and tomatoes.

Creamy Turkey Burgers

MAKES 6 BURGERS

I like to add a twist to my burgers. In this one, the unique combination of cream cheese and sweet pickles gives the burgers a kind of sweet-and-sour aura. The chopped green onion adds some color.

VARIATION
Use herb-flavored cream cheese for added flavor.

✦ Preheat barbecue

1 lb	lean ground turkey	500 g
¼ cup	soda cracker crumbs	50 mL
¼ cup	finely minced sweet gherkins	50 mL
¼ cup	cream cheese, at room temperature	50 mL
1	green onion, chopped	1
2	cloves garlic, minced	2
1	egg, beaten	1
½ tsp	paprika	2 mL
¼ tsp	salt	1 mL
¼ tsp	freshly ground black pepper	1 mL
6	hamburger buns, split and lightly toasted	6

1. In a large bowl, combine ground turkey, soda cracker crumbs, gherkins, cream cheese, green onion, garlic, egg, paprika, salt and pepper. Mix well. Shape into 6 ½-inch (1 cm) thick patties.

2. Place on preheated barbecue over medium heat. Cook, turning once, for 7 to 8 minutes per side or until no longer pink.

3. Serve in toasted buns. Garnish with your favorite toppings, such as Dijon mustard, lettuce, pickles and tomatoes.

Pimento Turkey Burgers

MAKES 6 BURGERS

This burger is bursting with color and flavor thanks to the green olives with pimento and the Dijon mayonnaise. For a change, consider serving the burgers on whole wheat buns.

VARIATION

In place of Dijon mayonnaise, stir together 1 tbsp (15 mL) each Dijon mustard and mayonnaise.

✦ Preheat barbecue

1 lb	lean ground turkey	500 g
¼ cup	dry bread crumbs	50 mL
¼ cup	chopped green olives with pimento	50 mL
2 tbsp	chopped onion	25 mL
2 tbsp	Dijon mayonnaise (see Variation, left)	25 mL
2	cloves garlic, minced	2
1	egg, beaten	1
¼ tsp	salt	1 mL
¼ tsp	freshly ground black pepper	1 mL
6	hamburger buns, split and lightly toasted	6

1. In a large bowl, combine ground turkey, bread crumbs, olives, onion, Dijon mayonnaise, garlic, egg, salt and pepper. Mix well. Shape into 6 ½-inch (1 cm) thick patties.

2. Place on preheated barbecue over medium heat. Cook, turning once, for 7 to 8 minutes per side or until no longer pink.

3. Serve in toasted buns. Garnish with your favorite toppings, such as lettuce, pickles, purple onion and tomatoes.

One-Dish Meals

Cabbage Rolls

SERVES 6 TO 8

This quintessential comfort food is more traditional than trendy — but why mess with down-home perfection?

VARIATION
Use vegetarian ground beef replacement or ground turkey instead of ground beef.

✦ Preheat oven to 350°F (180°C)
✦ 14-cup (3.5 L) casserole, greased

1 tbsp	vegetable oil	15 mL
1	onion, chopped	1
4	cloves garlic, minced	4
1 lb	lean ground beef	500 g
½ tsp	salt	2 mL
¼ tsp	freshly ground black pepper	1 mL
2 cups	cooked rice (about ½ cup/125 mL uncooked)	500 mL
1	can (28 oz/796 mL) tomato juice, divided	1
1	medium cabbage (about 1 to 1½ lbs/500 to 750 g)	1
2 tbsp	packed brown sugar	25 mL
1 tbsp	cider vinegar	15 mL
¼ tsp	garlic powder	1 mL
	Salt and freshly ground black pepper, to taste	

1. In a large nonstick skillet, heat oil over medium heat. Sauté onion and garlic for 3 minutes or until onion is softened.

2. Add ground beef and brown, breaking up meat, for 7 minutes or until no longer pink. Stir in salt and pepper. Add rice and 1 cup (250 mL) of the tomato juice. Simmer for 10 minutes or until thickened.

3. Meanwhile, cut out core of cabbage and remove any damaged outer leaves. In a large pot of boiling water, boil cabbage, covered, for 7 minutes or until leaves are tender. Carefully remove cabbage. Drain and let cool slightly. Separate leaves.

4. Place about 2 tbsp (25 mL) of the filling in middle of each cabbage leaf. Fold in edges and roll up. Place seam side down, in prepared casserole, layering as necessary.

5. To remaining tomato juice, add brown sugar, cider vinegar, garlic powder and salt and pepper. Pour over cabbage rolls. Bake in preheated oven for $1\frac{1}{2}$ hours or until leaves are tender and sauce is bubbling.

MAKE AHEAD
Cabbage rolls can be cooled, covered and frozen for up to 1 month. Let thaw overnight in the refrigerator. Reheat in 350°F (180°C) oven for 45 minutes.

Easy Cabbage Rolls

If you crave the comfort of cabbage rolls in a hurry, this recipe is for you. Layering all the components — rather than wrapping and rolling — cuts down on cooking time but not on flavor.

TIP

To shorten baking time, boil shredded cabbage for 7 to 10 minutes or until tender. Prepare as directed but bake for only 30 minutes.

VARIATION

In place of stewed tomatoes, tomato paste, tomato juice, sugar and caraway seeds, use 1 can (10 oz/284 mL) tomato soup. Mix about one-third of the can with meat and rice, reserving the remainder to pour over top layer of cabbage.

◆ Preheat oven to 350°F (180°C)
◆ 12-cup (3 L) casserole, greased

1	can (19 oz/540 mL) stewed tomatoes	1
1	can (5½ oz/156 mL) tomato paste	1
½ cup	tomato juice	125 mL
2 tsp	caraway seeds	10 mL
1 tsp	granulated sugar	5 mL
1 tbsp	vegetable oil	15 mL
1	medium onion, chopped	1
2	cloves garlic, minced	2
	Salt and freshly ground black pepper, to taste	
1 lb	lean ground beef	500 g
1 cup	cooked long-grain white rice (about ¼ cup/50 mL uncooked)	250 mL
6 cups	coarsely shredded cabbage (about 1 medium)	1.5 L

1. In a medium saucepan over medium-high heat, combine tomatoes, tomato paste, tomato juice, caraway seeds and sugar. Bring to a boil. Reduce heat and simmer for 15 minutes or until tomatoes are broken down and sauce is thickened.

2. Meanwhile, in a skillet, heat oil over medium heat. Sauté onion and garlic for 2 minutes or until softened. Add ground beef and brown, breaking up meat, for 7 minutes or until no longer pink. Season with salt and pepper.

3. Remove 1½ cups (375 mL) of the tomato sauce from saucepan. Set aside. Add meat and rice to saucepan. Stir until well combined.

4. Place cabbage in a large saucepan and cover with boiling water. Let stand for 5 minutes. Drain.

5. Place half the cabbage in bottom of prepared casserole. Cover with meat mixture. Top with remaining cabbage. Pour reserved tomato sauce over top. Cover and bake in preheated oven for 1 hour or until leaves are tender and sauce is bubbling.

Chorizo Sausage and Black Bean Burritos

SERVES 4

The chorizo sausage gives this dish zing. For a milder rendition, replace sausage with ground beef.

VARIATIONS

Use Italian sausage in place of chorizo.

Use Cheddar cheese in place of Monterey Jack.

♦ Preheat oven to 350°F (180°C)
♦ 13-by 9-inch (3 L) baking dish, lightly sprayed

8 oz	soft chorizo sausage, casings removed	250 g
1	small onion, chopped	1
2	cloves garlic, minced	2
1 cup	tomato sauce	250 mL
1	can (19 oz/540 mL) black beans, drained and rinsed	1
½ tsp	ground cumin	2 mL
¼ cup	chopped fresh cilantro	50 mL
1 tsp	freshly squeezed lime juice	5 mL
8	large (10-inch/25 cm) flour tortillas	8
1½ cups	shredded Monterey Jack cheese	375 mL
	Salsa	
	Sour cream	

1. In a large skillet over medium heat, cook sausage, breaking up meat, for 7 minutes or until no longer pink.

2. Add onion and garlic. Sauté for 3 minutes or until onion is softened. Add tomato sauce, black beans and cumin. Simmer for 15 minutes. Stir in cilantro and lime juice.

3. Spread about ⅓ cup (75 mL) of the mixture onto center of 1 tortilla. Fold up bottom then sides. Roll up until filling is completely enclosed. Place, seam side down, in prepared baking dish. Continue with remaining tortillas and filling.

4. Sprinkle cheese evenly over burritos. Bake, uncovered, in preheated oven for 12 to 15 minutes or until cheese is melted and filling is hot. Serve with salsa and sour cream.

MAKE AHEAD
Prepare burritos up to the end of Step 3. Cover and refrigerate. Before reheating, let stand at room temperature for 15 minutes. Top with cheese and heat for 20 minutes or until heated through.

Ground Beef Hash Bake

SERVES 4 TO 6

The simple frozen hash brown is given a boost in this one-dish wonder thanks to the ground beef, salsa and my secret ingredient — sharp cold-pack Cheddar. The next time you require a large dinner in a dish, remember this simple solution.

TIPS

Sharp cold-pack Cheddar is sold in plastic containers alongside other processed cheese. It has an intense flavor and melts marvelously. Always grate directly from refrigerator.

This recipe doubles easily. To do so, double all ingredients except mushroom soup.

VARIATIONS

Use Italian sausage, casings removed and meat crumbled, in place of ground beef and salsa. Sauté as directed until no longer pink. Serve this version for brunch.

Use old Cheddar in place of sharp cold-pack Cheddar.

✦ Preheat oven to 375°F (190°C)
✦ 13-by 9-inch (3 L) baking dish, lightly sprayed

1 tsp	olive oil	5 mL
½	onion, chopped	½
1	clove garlic, minced	1
8 oz	lean ground beef	250 g
1 tbsp	hot salsa	15 mL
1 lb	frozen hash browns	500 g
1	can (10 oz/284 mL) condensed cream of mushroom soup, undiluted	1
1 cup	grated cold-pack sharp Cheddar cheese (see Tips, left)	250 mL
1 cup	sour cream Salt and freshly ground black pepper, to taste	250 mL

1. In a nonstick skillet, heat oil over medium heat. Sauté onion and garlic for 3 minutes or until onion is softened.

2. Add ground beef and brown, breaking up meat, for 7 minutes or until no longer pink. Stir in salsa.

3. In a large bowl, combine cooked ground beef mixture, hash browns, mushroom soup, Cheddar cheese and sour cream. Season with salt and pepper. Mix well.

4. Spoon into prepared baking dish. Bake in preheated oven for 35 to 40 minutes or until browned on top.

MAKE AHEAD

Prepare in advance, baking for 30 minutes. Let cool, cover and refrigerate for up to 2 days. To reheat, bake in 350°F (180°C) oven for 20 minutes.

Seven-Layer Dinner

SERVES 4

*For as long as ladies'
auxiliaries have been
putting out cookbooks,
this ground beef recipe
has appeared in various
guises. You layer your
staple ingredients in a
casserole, pour a can of
tomato soup over the
whole lot and forget
about it while it slowly
bakes in the oven at a
moderate temperature.
But who has an hour and
half for a basic dinner
these days? My version
gives the seven-layer
dinner a new spin by
relying on preformed
meatballs and the handy
microwave (what would
our grandmothers say?).
I've also injected additional
seasoning to give it a little
more oomph.*

TIP

If you prefer to bake
this in a regular oven,
place all ingredients in
casserole and bake in
350°F (180°C) oven
for 1 hour.

VARIATION

In place of ground beef
meatballs, use plain
ground beef. Cook as
directed.

◆ Microwave-safe 10-cup (2.5 L) casserole

1 lb	lean ground beef, formed into 24 meatballs	500 g
¼ tsp	salt	1 mL
¼ tsp	freshly ground black pepper	1 mL
1 tbsp	steak sauce (such as HP Sauce)	15 mL
2	potatoes, peeled and thinly sliced	2
1	small onion, thinly sliced	1
½	green bell pepper, cut into strips	½
½	red bell pepper, cut into strips	½
2	carrots, peeled and sliced	2
1	stalk celery, sliced	1
1	can (10 oz/284 mL) condensed tomato soup, undiluted	1
½ cup	water	125 mL
¼ tsp	garlic powder	1 mL
3	drops hot pepper sauce	3

1. Place meatballs in casserole. Season with salt and
   pepper. Microwave on High for 3 minutes. Drain
   off excess fat. Turn meatballs and add steak sauce.
   Microwave on High for 3 minutes longer. Drain
   off fat and turn meatballs.

2. Layer potatoes, onion, green and red peppers,
   carrots and celery over meatballs.

3. In a bowl, mix soup with water. Season with garlic
   powder and hot pepper sauce. Pour over casserole.
   Microwave on High for 20 minutes or until meatballs
   are no longer pink and vegetables are tender. Serve
   immediately.

Lamb Meatball, Eggplant and Zucchini Casserole

SERVES 4 TO 6

These flavorful lamb meatballs marry well with eggplant and zucchini. The beauty of this casserole is that you can prepare it in advance to serve later in the day.

TIPS

There's no need to add oil to the skillet when frying the lamb meatballs.

In place of fresh parsley in the meatballs, use ½ tsp (2 mL) dried parsley flakes.

VARIATION

Use ground beef in place of lamb.

- ✦ Preheat oven to 400°F (200°C)
- ✦ Baking sheet, lightly sprayed
- ✦ 10-cup (2.5 L) casserole

1	can (28 oz/796 mL) tomatoes, including juice	1
1 tbsp	cider vinegar	15 mL
1½ tsp	packed brown sugar	7 mL
1 tsp	cumin seeds	5 mL
	Salt and freshly ground black pepper, to taste	
3	drops hot pepper sauce	3
2 tbsp	chopped fresh parsley	25 mL
1 lb	ground lamb	500 g
1½ tsp	chopped fresh parsley	7 mL
½ tsp	ground cumin	2 mL
½ tsp	salt	2 mL
¼ tsp	freshly ground black pepper	1 mL
¼ tsp	ground coriander	1 mL
⅛ tsp	ground cinnamon	0.5 mL
1	large onion, sliced	1
2	cloves garlic, minced	2
1	zucchini, sliced	1
1	eggplant, peeled and thinly sliced	1
	Cooked rice	

1. In a medium saucepan over medium-high heat, bring tomatoes with juice, cider vinegar, brown sugar, cumin seeds, salt, pepper and hot pepper sauce to a boil. Break up tomatoes with a fork. Reduce heat to low, cover and simmer for 15 minutes. Add 2 tbsp (25 mL) fresh parsley and simmer for 5 minutes longer or until thickened.

2. Meanwhile, in a medium bowl, combine ground lamb, 1½ tsp (7 mL) parsley, ground cumin, salt, pepper, coriander and cinnamon. Form into about 18 1-inch (2.5 cm) meatballs.

3. In a nonstick skillet, brown meatballs for 8 minutes, turning to brown all sides. Remove with slotted spoon and drain on paper towel.

4. Add onion, garlic and zucchini to skillet. Sauté for 3 minutes or until browned.

5. Meanwhile, place eggplant slices on prepared baking sheet. Bake in preheated oven, turning once, for 10 minutes or until lightly browned.

6. In casserole, layer half each of the eggplant, zucchini mixture, meatballs and tomato sauce. Repeat layers.

7. Bake, covered, in 350°F (180°C) oven for 30 minutes or until heated through. Serve over cooked rice.

MAKE AHEAD
Prepare earlier in the day up to the end of Step 6. Bake as directed just before serving.

Mexican Chicken Casserole

SERVES 6

This dish, with its built-in cornbread topping, looks good enough to serve to company but is simple enough to make for a nice family meal.

VARIATION

For a less spicy version, omit cayenne pepper and pickled jalapeño peppers.

◆ Preheat oven to 350°F (180°C)
◆ 12-cup (3 L) casserole

1 tbsp	vegetable oil	15 mL
1	onion, chopped	1
1	clove garlic, minced	1
1	stalk celery, chopped	1
1/2	red bell pepper, chopped	1/2
1/2	green bell pepper, chopped	1/2
1 1/2 lbs	lean ground chicken	750 g
1 1/2 tsp	chili powder	7 mL
1/2 tsp	ground cumin	2 mL
1/4 tsp	cayenne pepper	1 mL
1/4 tsp	salt	1 mL
1/2 cup	frozen corn kernels	125 mL
1/2 cup	chicken stock	125 mL

TOPPING

1 cup	all-purpose flour	250 mL
3/4 cup	cornmeal	175 mL
1 tbsp	baking powder	15 mL
1/2 tsp	salt	2 mL
1/8 tsp	freshly ground black pepper	0.5 mL
1 1/2 tbsp	butter	22 mL
2	eggs, beaten	2
2/3 cup	milk	150 mL
2 tbsp	chopped pickled jalapeño peppers	25 mL
1/4 cup	chopped fresh cilantro	50 mL
1 cup	finely shredded Cheddar cheese	250 mL

1. In a nonstick skillet, heat oil over medium heat. Sauté onion, garlic, celery and red and green peppers for 5 minutes or until vegetables are softened.

2. Add ground chicken. Season with chili powder, cumin, cayenne and salt. Brown, breaking up chicken, for 7 minutes or until no longer pink.

3. Place chicken and vegetable mixture in bottom of casserole. Stir in frozen corn kernels. Pour in chicken stock. Mix well.

4. *Topping:* In a bowl, combine flour, cornmeal, baking powder, salt and pepper. Cut in butter with a pastry blender or two knives until mixture resembles coarse crumbs. Beat together eggs and milk. Pour into cornmeal mixture and blend well. Stir in jalapeños and cilantro.

5. Spoon topping over chicken mixture. Sprinkle with Cheddar cheese. Bake in preheated oven for 30 minutes or until top is golden.

Lamb Moussaka

This superb Greek specialty will wow your guests at a dinner party or casual get-together. And the aroma is amazing, too!

- ✦ Preheat oven to 425°F (220°C)
- ✦ 2 baking sheets, lightly sprayed
- ✦ 13-by 9-inch (3 L) glass baking dish, lightly sprayed

1	large eggplant, peeled and sliced $\frac{1}{2}$ inch (1 cm) thick (about 1 lb/500 g)	1
	Salt	
1 tbsp	olive oil	15 mL
1	onion, chopped	1
2	cloves garlic, minced	2
1 lb	ground lamb	500 g
1 lb	potatoes, peeled and thinly sliced (about 4 medium)	500 g
1	can (28 oz/796 mL) diced tomatoes, including juice	1
$\frac{1}{4}$ tsp	ground cloves	1 mL
$\frac{1}{4}$ tsp	ground cinnamon	1 mL
$\frac{1}{4}$ tsp	ground allspice	1 mL
	Salt and freshly ground black pepper, to taste	

BÉCHAMEL SAUCE

2 tbsp	butter	25 mL
$\frac{1}{4}$ cup	all-purpose flour	50 mL
2 cups	warm milk	500 mL
6 tbsp	freshly grated Parmesan cheese, divided	90 mL
Pinch	ground nutmeg	Pinch
2	eggs, beaten	2

1. Sprinkle eggplant slices with salt. Drain in colander in sink for 15 minutes.

2. In a Dutch oven or large saucepan, heat oil over medium heat. Sauté onion for 3 minutes. Add garlic and sauté for 1 minute longer.

3. Add ground lamb and brown, breaking up meat, for 7 minutes or until no longer pink. Drain off excess fat.

4. Meanwhile, wipe off eggplant slices with paper towel. Place eggplant slices in a single layer on one of the prepared baking sheets. Place potato slices in a single layer on the other baking sheet. Bake in preheated oven for 10 minutes, turning once, or until lightly browned. Set aside. Reduce oven temperature to 375°F (190°C).

5. Once lamb is cooked through, drain fat from lamb (ideally in a colander in sink). Return lamb to Dutch oven or saucepan. Increase heat to medium-high. Add diced tomatoes, cloves, cinnamon, allspice and salt and pepper and bring to a boil. Reduce heat to low and simmer, stirring occasionally and breaking up tomatoes, for 30 minutes or until thickened.

6. *Béchamel Sauce:* In a saucepan over low heat, melt butter. Add flour and stir for 1 minute. Slowly pour in warm milk and cook, stirring, for 2 minutes or until thickened. Add ¼ cup (50 mL) of the Parmesan cheese and nutmeg. Cook, stirring, for 1 minute longer or until blended. Whisk in beaten eggs, stirring until blended.

7. Arrange potatoes in a single layer on bottom of prepared baking dish. Layer half of the eggplant in a single layer on top. Spread all of the meat mixture over eggplant. Top with remaining eggplant (and any remaining potato slices) in a single layer. Spread Béchamel Sauce over top. Sprinkle with remaining Parmesan cheese. Bake in 375°F (190°C) oven for 60 minutes or until hot and bubbling.

MAKE AHEAD

Prepare moussaka (except for Béchamel Sauce) up to 1 day in advance. Cover and refrigerate. To serve, prepare sauce and pour over meat and vegetable layers. Reheat in 350°F (180°C) oven for 40 minutes or until heated through.

Stuffed Peppers

SERVES 6

This family favorite is an excellent make-ahead meal. The stuffed peppers are even better the next day! And they freeze well, too. This dish is especially wonderful to make when green and red bell peppers are abundant (and cheap) at the supermarket or farmer's market.

TIP

Don't discard the pepper tops. If there's any additional beef and rice mixture, simply dish it onto the tops and bake with the stuffed peppers.

VARIATION

Use other colors of peppers in combination with the green peppers. Sweet red peppers are excellent.

✦ Preheat oven to 350°F (180°C)
✦ Microwave-safe 12-cup (3 L) casserole

1 tbsp	olive oil	15 mL
1	onion, chopped	1
2	cloves garlic, minced	2
1 lb	lean ground beef	500 g
1	can (14 oz/398 mL) tomato sauce	1
1½ cups	stewed tomatoes	375 mL
1 tbsp	tomato paste	15 mL
1 tsp	sweet paprika	5 mL
4	drops hot pepper sauce	4
	Salt and freshly ground black pepper, to taste	
2 cups	cooked long-grain white rice (½ cup/125 mL uncooked)	500 mL
6	large green bell peppers	6
1 cup	shredded Cheddar cheese	250 mL

1. In a large skillet, heat oil over medium heat. Sauté onion and garlic for 3 minutes or until onions are softened.

2. Add ground beef and brown, breaking up meat, for 7 minutes or until no longer pink.

3. Increase heat to medium-high. Add tomato sauce, stewed tomatoes, tomato paste, paprika and hot pepper sauce. Bring to a boil. Season with salt and pepper. Add cooked rice. Reduce heat to medium-low and simmer, uncovered, stirring occasionally, for 20 minutes or until thickened.

4. Meanwhile, cut tops off green peppers and remove stems. Discard seeds. Place peppers and tops (see Tip, far left) in casserole. Pour in ½ cup (125 mL) water. Cover loosely with waxed paper and microwave on High for 5 minutes or until peppers just begin to soften.

5. Drain water from casserole. With peppers standing upright in casserole, fill each to the top with ground meat and rice mixture, packing lightly as necessary. Sprinkle cheese on each. Bake in preheated oven for 30 minutes or until cheese is melted and mixture is bubbling.

MAKE AHEAD
Prepare up to the end of Step 3 and refrigerate filling, covered, for up to 2 days. (Or peppers can be filled, baked and refrigerated for up to 2 days.) Baked stuffed peppers can also be frozen in an airtight container for up to 2 weeks. If planning to freeze, do not add cheese.

Taco Salad Casserole

Children can help prepare this kid-friendly meal, making it an even speedier suppertime solution. Have them slice vegetables, shred cheese and assemble their own plates of Taco Salad Casserole.

VARIATION
Instead of homemade Taco Seasoning Mix, use half a store-bought packet.

✦ Preheat oven to 350°F (180°C)
✦ 8-cup (2 L) casserole, lightly sprayed

1 tsp	vegetable oil	5 mL
1	small onion, finely chopped	1
1	clove garlic, minced	1
1 lb	lean ground beef	500 g
¾ cup	water	175 mL
1 tbsp	Taco Seasoning Mix (see recipe, right)	15 mL
1 cup	medium salsa	250 mL
1 cup	shredded Cheddar cheese	250 mL
¼ cup	sliced black olives	50 mL
2 cups	shredded lettuce	500 mL
1	tomato, diced	1
½	green bell pepper, thinly sliced	½
	Sour cream	
	Chopped green onions	
	Tortilla chips	

1. In a skillet, heat oil over medium heat. Sauté onion and garlic for 3 minutes or until softened.

2. Add ground beef and brown, breaking up meat, for 7 minutes or until no longer pink. Add water and Taco Seasoning Mix. Simmer for 10 minutes to allow flavors to blend.

3. Spread beef mixture in bottom of prepared casserole. Top with salsa. Sprinkle with Cheddar cheese, then olives. Bake in preheated oven for 30 minutes or until bubbling.

4. Divide the casserole into 4 servings. Top each with lettuce, tomato and green pepper. Serve with sour cream, chopped green onions, additional cheese, if desired, and tortilla chips.

MAKE AHEAD
Prepare the ground beef in advance. Before serving, add remaining ingredients and bake as directed.

Taco Seasoning Mix

MAKES ABOUT ⅓ CUP (75 ML)

TIP

Coarse garlic powder is available at bulk food stores and other specialty stores. If unavailable, use fine garlic powder in its place.

2 tbsp	dried onion flakes	25 mL
2 tbsp	chili powder	25 mL
2 tsp	cornstarch	10 mL
1½ tsp	ground cumin	7 mL
1½ tsp	salt	7 mL
1½ tsp	coarse garlic powder (see Tip, left)	7 mL
1½ tsp	hot pepper flakes	7 mL
1½ tsp	dry beef bouillon powder	7 mL
¾ tsp	dried oregano leaves	4 mL

1. In a bowl, combine dried onion flakes, chili powder, cornstarch, ground cumin, salt, garlic powder, hot pepper flakes, bouillon powder and dried oregano. Mix well. Keep in a jar with a tight-fitting lid or resealable bag in a cool cupboard for up to 3 months.

2. *To use:* 2 tbsp (25 mL) mix plus ¾ cup (175 mL) water equals 1 package of store-bought taco seasoning mix. Add to 1 lb (500 g) drained browned ground meat. Simmer for 10 minutes.

Tacos

SERVES 6 TO 8

This all-time favorite is made even better by using your own homemade Taco Seasoning Mix. It will keep for six months in a dry, cool place. Tacos are great munchies for football fans during half-time. Double the recipe for a large crowd.

TIP
Place taco toppings in a large compartmentalized serving dish.

VARIATION
Use ground chicken in place of ground beef but add an additional ¼ cup (50 mL) water to the mixture.

✦ Preheat oven to 350°F (180°C)

1 tbsp	vegetable oil	15 mL
1	small onion, chopped	1
2	cloves garlic, minced	2
1 lb	lean ground beef	500 g
¾ cup	water	175 mL
2 tbsp	Taco Seasoning Mix (see recipe, page 101)	25 mL
12	hard taco shells	12
2 cups	shredded lettuce	500 mL
1	large tomato, chopped	1
¼ cup	sliced black olives	50 mL
1 cup	shredded Cheddar cheese	250 mL
	Salsa	
	Sour cream	

1. In a large skillet, heat oil over medium heat. Sauté onion and garlic for 3 minutes or until onion is softened.

2. Add ground beef and brown, breaking up meat, for 7 minutes or until no longer pink. Add water and Taco Seasoning Mix. Increase heat to medium-high. Bring to a boil. Reduce heat to medium-low and simmer for 10 minutes, stirring occasionally, until thickened.

3. Heat taco shells in preheated oven for 5 minutes.

4. Fill individual bowls with lettuce, chopped tomato, sliced olives, Cheddar cheese, salsa and sour cream. Spoon beef mixture into hot tacos. Place tacos and accompaniments on table buffet-style for everyone to top as desired.

MAKE AHEAD
Prepare beef mixture up to 1 day in advance. Let cool, cover and refrigerate. Reheat in microwave for 7 minutes or until heated through. Prepare vegetables and refrigerate until ready to serve.

Turkey Basil Casserole

SERVES 4 TO 6

If you have fussy eaters in your family, this casserole offers ample opportunity to sneak in extra vegetables — without their knowing it.

TIP

This dish freezes well. Prepare as directed and freeze in an airtight container for up to 2 weeks.

VARIATION

Top with shredded mozzarella cheese before baking in oven.

◆ Preheat oven to 350°F (180°C)
◆ 12-cup (3 L) casserole

1 tbsp	olive oil	15 mL
1	onion, chopped	1
2	cloves garlic, minced	2
1 lb	lean ground turkey	500 g
1/4 tsp	salt	1 mL
1/4 tsp	freshly ground black pepper	1 mL
1/2	yellow bell pepper, chopped	1/2
1/2	red bell pepper, chopped	1/2
1	can (28 oz/796 mL) stewed tomatoes, including juice	1
1/4 cup	chopped fresh parsley	50 mL
1 tbsp	chopped fresh basil	15 mL
2 cups	frozen snow peas	500 mL
2 cups	rotini pasta	500 mL

1. In a large skillet, heat oil over medium heat. Sauté onion and garlic for 3 minutes or until onion is softened.

2. Add ground turkey. Season with salt and pepper. Brown, breaking up turkey, for 7 minutes or until no longer pink. Add yellow and red peppers. Sauté for 2 minutes or until tender.

3. Pour in stewed tomatoes with juice, parsley and basil. Bring to a boil. Reduce heat to medium-low and simmer, stirring occasionally and breaking up tomatoes, for 15 minutes or until thickened. Add snow peas. Sauté for 2 minutes.

4. Meanwhile, in a large saucepan of boiling salted water, cook pasta for 8 minutes or until al dente. Drain.

5. Transfer pasta to large casserole. Top with turkey mixture and tomato sauce. Stir well. Bake in preheated oven for 20 minutes or until heated through.

Veal Casserole

SERVES 4 TO 6

The inclusion of red wine and tomatoes, along with the usual osso buco seasonings, makes this a comfort food casserole with a touch of class.

TIP
Use 4 to 6 cups
(1 to 1.5 L) leftover
mashed potatoes.

✦ Preheat oven to 350°F (180°C)
✦ 10-cup (2.5 L) casserole

1 tbsp	olive oil	15 mL
1	onion, chopped	1
2	cloves garlic, minced	2
1 lb	lean ground veal	500 g
½ tsp	salt	2 mL
¼ tsp	freshly ground black pepper	1 mL
¼ tsp	dried thyme leaves	1 mL
1½ cups	canned whole tomatoes, including juice	375 mL
1	can (5½ oz/156 mL) tomato paste	1
½ cup	dry red wine	125 mL
1 tsp	Worcestershire sauce	5 mL
½ tsp	dried oregano leaves	2 mL
½ tsp	granulated sugar	2 mL
1	bay leaf	1
1½ lbs	potatoes, peeled and quartered	750 g
1 tbsp	butter	15 mL
¼ cup	warm milk	50 mL
	Salt and freshly ground black pepper, to taste	

1. In a nonstick skillet, heat oil over medium heat. Sauté onion and garlic for 3 minutes or until softened.

2. Add ground veal and brown, breaking up meat, for 7 minutes or until no longer pink. Season with salt, pepper and thyme.

3. Add tomatoes with juice, tomato paste, wine, Worcestershire sauce, oregano, sugar and bay leaf. Increase heat to medium-high and bring to a boil. Reduce heat to medium-low and simmer for 20 minutes or until thickened. Remove bay leaf.

4. Meanwhile, in a large saucepan of boiling salted water, boil potatoes for 20 minutes or until tender. Drain. Mash with butter, warm milk, salt and pepper.

5. Spread veal mixture in bottom of casserole. Spread mashed potatoes on top. Bake in preheated oven for 30 minutes or until heated through.

Meat Loaves
& Meatballs

Tried-and-True Meat Loaf

SERVES 4 TO 6

This traditional meat loaf recipe comes from recipe tester Cheryl Warkentin. It has become her family's favorite, especially when served with mashed potatoes and salad.

TIP
Oats give the meat loaf a slightly crunchy texture.

VARIATION
Use coarse fresh bread crumbs in place of oats.

◆ Preheat oven to 400°F (200°C)
◆ 9-by 5-inch (1.5 L) metal loaf pan, sprayed

1½ lbs	lean ground beef	750 g
1 cup	milk	250 mL
¾ cup	quick-cooking oats	175 mL
2 tbsp	minced onion	25 mL
¼ tsp	salt	1 mL
¼ tsp	freshly ground black pepper	1 mL
1 cup	ketchup	250 mL
½ cup	water	125 mL
¼ cup	minced onion	50 mL
3 tbsp	white vinegar	45 mL
2 tbsp	packed brown sugar	25 mL
2 tbsp	Worcestershire sauce	25 mL

1. In a large bowl, combine ground beef, milk, oats, 2 tbsp (25 mL) onion, salt and pepper. Mix well.

2. Pack loosely into prepared loaf pan. Bake in preheated oven for 10 minutes.

3. Meanwhile, in a bowl, combine ketchup, water, ¼ cup (50 mL) onion, vinegar, brown sugar and Worcestershire sauce. Pour sauce over meat loaf.

4. Bake for 75 to 80 minutes longer, checking after 60 minutes, or until thermometer inserted in center registers 160°F (71°C). Let stand for 5 minutes. Drain off excess liquid before slicing.

Scalloped Potato Meat Loaf

SERVES 4

This kid-friendly dinner combines two favorite comfort foods — scalloped potatoes and meat loaf — in one sensational savory supper. My youngest son, Evan, 11, gives this dish two thumbs up!

TIP

Use prepared chili sauce in place of spicy or regular ketchup.

VARIATION

Use low-fat mushroom soup.

✦ Preheat oven to 375°F (190°C)
✦ 9-inch (2.5 L) by 3-inch (7.5 cm) deep oval casserole, sprayed

1 lb	potatoes, peeled and thinly sliced, divided	500 g
1 cup	sliced onions	250 mL
	Salt and freshly ground black pepper, to taste	
1	can (10 oz/284 mL) condensed cream of mushroom soup, undiluted, divided	1
1 lb	lean ground beef	500 g
½ cup	dry bread crumbs	125 mL
1	egg	1
1	clove garlic, minced	1
½ cup	spicy or regular ketchup, divided	125 mL

1. Arrange half of the potatoes in a single layer in bottom of casserole. Top with half of the onions. Sprinkle with salt and pepper. Spread half of the mushroom soup over top. Repeat with remaining potatoes, onions and mushroom soup.

2. In a medium bowl, combine ground beef, bread crumbs, egg, garlic and ¼ cup (50 mL) of the ketchup. Mix well. Season with salt and pepper. Spread beef mixture over top of potato and onion layers. Spread remaining ketchup on top. Bake, uncovered, in preheated oven for 1 hour or until potatoes are tender and thermometer inserted in meat layer registers 160°F (71°C).

3. Turn oven to broiler, keeping oven door ajar. Broil meat loaf for 3 to 5 minutes or until top is browned. Let stand for 5 minutes. Drain off excess liquid before slicing.

Pesto Meat Loaf

SERVES 4

Pesto lovers will enjoy this rendition of meat loaf, featuring ground veal and ground beef and the much-loved combination of fresh basil, garlic, pine nuts, freshly grated Parmesan cheese and olive oil.

TIP
Serve Pesto Meat Loaf with pasta instead of the traditional mashed potatoes.

VARIATIONS
In place of pine nuts, use toasted slivered almonds.

Use ground chicken in place of ground beef and ground veal. If using chicken, add ¼ cup (50 mL) chicken stock to meat and pesto mixture.

+ Preheat oven to 350°F (180°C)
+ 9-by 5-inch (1.5 L) metal loaf pan, sprayed

2 tbsp	pine nuts	25 mL
3	cloves garlic	3
¼ cup	chopped fresh basil	50 mL
2 tbsp	freshly grated Parmesan cheese	25 mL
1 tbsp	olive oil	15 mL
8 oz	lean ground veal	250 g
8 oz	lean ground beef	250 g
½ cup	soda cracker crumbs	125 mL
1	egg, beaten	1
Topping		
¼ cup	ketchup	50 mL
1 tsp	chopped fresh basil	5 mL
⅛ tsp	dried onion flakes	0.5 mL

1. In a skillet over medium heat, brown pine nuts, stirring constantly, for 2 minutes or until browned. Remove from heat.

2. In a blender or food processor, mince garlic. Add basil, pine nuts, Parmesan cheese and oil. Process with three or four on/off pulses until puréed. (This mixture may be much drier than regular pesto because of the small amount of olive oil.)

3. In a large bowl, combine ground veal, ground beef, soda cracker crumbs, egg and pesto. Mix well. Pack into prepared loaf pan.

4. *Topping:* In a small bowl, combine ketchup, basil and onion flakes. Spread over meat loaf. Bake, uncovered, in preheated oven for 65 minutes or until thermometer inserted in center registers 160°F (71°C). Let stand for 5 minutes. Drain off excess liquid before slicing.

MAKE AHEAD
Prepare pesto up to 3 days in advance and refrigerate in a covered container.

Zippy Meat Loaf Muffins

MAKES 9 MUFFINS

Meat loaf gets a makeover when baked in muffin cups. This recipe is ideal for children's lunches or when you're cooking for one or two.

TIP
This recipe can easily be doubled.

VARIATION
Use your favorite meat loaf recipe and divide among muffin cups.

+ Preheat oven to 400°F (200°C)
+ Muffin tin, sprayed

1 lb	lean ground beef	500 g
1	egg, beaten	1
2	cloves garlic, minced	2
2	green onions, finely minced	2
½ cup	dry bread crumbs	125 mL
2 tbsp	ketchup	25 mL
1 tbsp	Worcestershire sauce	15 mL
1 tbsp	prepared mustard	15 mL
	Salt and freshly ground black pepper, to taste	
3 tbsp	prepared chili sauce	45 mL

1. In a large bowl, combine ground beef, egg, garlic, green onions, bread crumbs, ketchup, Worcestershire sauce and mustard. Mix well. Season with salt and pepper.

2. Form meat into 9 balls. Place each in prepared muffin tin. Brush with chili sauce. Fill unused muffin cups with water to prevent warping of pan.

3. Bake in preheated oven for 20 minutes or until no longer pink and thermometer inserted in center registers 160°F (71°C). Drain off any excess fat.

MAKE AHEAD
These meat loaf muffins freeze well. Let cool, then freeze in resealable bag for up to 1 month.

Wild Rice Chicken Loaf

SERVES 4

Mild ground chicken is upgraded with flavorful wild rice stuffing mix, white wine and toasted pine nuts.

TIP

To toast pine nuts, heat in nonstick skillet over medium heat, stirring constantly, for about 2 minutes or until lightly browned.

VARIATION

Use toasted slivered almonds in place of pine nuts.

+ Preheat oven to 350°F (180°C)
+ 9-by 5-inch (1.5 L) metal loaf pan, sprayed

1	box (4 oz/120 g) long-grain and wild rice stuffing mix	1
1 tbsp	olive oil	15 mL
1	shallot, chopped	1
1	clove garlic, minced	1
½ cup	sliced mushrooms	125 mL
½ cup	white wine	125 mL
1 lb	lean ground chicken	500 g
1	egg, beaten	1
	Salt and freshly ground black pepper, to taste	
2 tbsp	pine nuts, toasted (see Tip, left)	25 mL
¼ cup	chicken stock	50 mL

1. Prepare stuffing mixture according to package directions. Set aside.

2. In a nonstick skillet, heat oil over medium heat. Sauté shallot, garlic and mushrooms for 3 minutes. Add white wine and simmer for 5 minutes or until reduced by half. Add to stuffing mixture. Mix well.

3. In a medium bowl, combine ground chicken, egg, salt and pepper. Stir in mushroom mixture. Add pine nuts.

4. Pack into prepared loaf pan. Bake in preheated oven for 45 minutes. Pour chicken stock over loaf and bake for 30 minutes longer or until thermometer inserted in center registers 175°F (80°C). Let stand for 5 minutes. Drain off excess liquid before slicing.

Stuffed Turkey Meat Loaf

SERVES 4

This fabulous recipe combines stuffing and turkey all in one dish. Serve with cranberry sauce for a real Thanksgiving touch.

VARIATION
Use other stuffing mixes, such as wild rice or chicken stuffing mix.

✦ Preheat oven to 350°F (180°C)
✦ 9-by 5-inch (1.5 L) metal loaf pan, sprayed

1½ lbs	lean ground turkey	750 g
1	egg, beaten	1
½ cup	dry bread crumbs	125 mL
½ cup	chicken stock	125 ml
½ tsp	salt	2 mL
¼ tsp	garlic powder	1 mL
¼ tsp	freshly ground black pepper	1 mL
1	envelope (4 oz/120 g) turkey stuffing mix	1
1	package (1 oz/25 g) turkey gravy (yield 1 cup/250 mL)	1

1. In a mixing bowl, combine ground turkey, egg, bread crumbs, chicken stock, salt, garlic powder and pepper.

2. Pack about 1½ cups (375 mL) of the mixture in bottom of prepared loaf pan. Using 1 cup (250 mL) of the meat mixture, form a 2-inch (5 cm) wall around loaf pan, leaving a cavity in the center.

3. Prepare stuffing mix according to package directions. Spoon into ground turkey cavity, packing down to fit level with top of meat.

4. Press out remaining meat mixture in a single layer on waxed paper, roughly the same size as the loaf pan. Invert waxed paper over pan. Peel off paper and join top layer of meat with walls, tucking in meat as necessary. Bake, uncovered, in preheated oven for 45 minutes.

5. Meanwhile, prepare turkey gravy according to package directions. After 45 minutes, remove loaf. Pour gravy over top and bake for 20 minutes longer or until thermometer inserted in meat registers 175°F (80°C). Let stand for 5 minutes. Drain off excess liquid before slicing.

MAKE AHEAD
Prepare stuffing and gravy and refrigerate, covered, for up to 1 day. Reheat gravy before pouring over loaf.

Cranberry Turkey Loaf

SERVES 4

My friend Barb Altman shared this recipe, a family favorite. The sunflower seeds and cranberries supply a unique texture to the tasty meat loaf, and the glaze finishes it off beautifully.

TIP
If desired, this recipe can be doubled for two regular-size meat loaves, or one larger meat loaf baked in a 13-by 9-inch (3 L) loaf pan.

VARIATION
Omit fresh parsley and add ¼ tsp (1 mL) poultry seasoning.

✦ Preheat oven to 325°F (160°C)
✦ 9-by 5-inch (1.5 L) metal loaf pan, sprayed

1¼ lbs	lean ground turkey	625 g
2	eggs, beaten	2
1 cup	fresh bread crumbs	250 mL
¼ cup	chopped fresh parsley	50 mL
¼ cup	water	50 mL
3 tbsp	dried cranberries	45 mL
2 tbsp	sunflower seeds, roasted	25 mL
1½ tsp	sesame seeds	7 mL
2	cloves garlic, minced	2
½ tsp	salt	2 mL
¼ tsp	freshly ground black pepper	1 mL

GLAZE

⅓ cup	prepared chili sauce	75 mL
⅓ cup	cranberry sauce	75 mL

1. In a large bowl, combine ground turkey, eggs, bread crumbs, parsley, water, cranberries, sunflower seeds, sesame seeds, garlic, salt and pepper. Mix well.

2. Pack into prepared loaf pan. Bake in preheated oven for 40 minutes.

3. *Glaze:* Meanwhile, in a small saucepan over low heat, combine chili and cranberry sauces for 5 minutes or until heated through. If sauce is too thick, add additional chili sauce.

4. Pour glaze over loaf. Bake for 30 minutes longer or until thermometer inserted in center registers 175°F (80°C). Let stand for 5 minutes. Drain off excess liquid before slicing.

"Dill"icious Turkey Meat Loaf

SERVES 4

Serve this dilly dish with mashed potatoes and steamed broccoli for a family-friendly weeknight supper.

TIP
Be sure to mince the onion finely.

VARIATION
Use 2 tbsp (25 mL) Dijon or whole grain mustard if you only have one of them on hand.

✦ Preheat oven to 325°F (160°C)
✦ 9-by 5-inch (1.5 L) metal loaf pan, lightly sprayed

1 lb	lean ground turkey	500 g
1	egg, beaten	1
1	small onion, finely minced	1
2	cloves garlic, minced	2
¼ cup	dry bread crumbs	50 mL
¼ cup	chopped fresh dill	50 mL
½ cup	chicken stock, divided	125 mL
1 tbsp	Dijon mustard	15 mL
¼ tsp	salt	1 mL
¼ tsp	freshly ground black pepper	1 mL
1 tbsp	whole grain mustard	15 mL

1. In a large bowl, combine ground turkey, egg, onion, garlic, bread crumbs, dill, ¼ cup (50 mL) of the chicken stock and Dijon mustard. Season with salt and pepper. Mix well.

2. Pack mixture into prepared loaf pan. Pour remaining chicken stock over top. Bake in preheated oven for 60 minutes.

3. Spread mustard over top. Bake for 10 minutes longer or until thermometer inserted in center registers 175°F (80°C). Let stand for 5 minutes. Drain off excess liquid before slicing.

Hawaiian Meatballs

SERVES 4

These sweet-and-sour meatballs are spectacular thanks to the addition of pineapple tidbits and green and red bell peppers.

TIP
Serve over white rice with a side dish of steamed broccoli.

MEATBALLS

1 lb	lean ground beef	500 g
½	small onion, finely minced	½
2	cloves garlic, minced	2
1	egg, beaten	1
⅓ cup	soda cracker crumbs	75 mL
¼ tsp	salt	1 mL
¼ tsp	freshly ground black pepper	1 mL
2 tbsp	olive oil for frying (approx.)	25 mL

SAUCE

1	can (19 oz/540 mL) pineapple tidbits, drained and juice reserved	1
1 cup	water	250 mL
¼ cup	packed brown sugar	50 mL
¼ cup	cider vinegar	50 mL
2 tbsp	soy sauce	25 mL
2 tbsp	cornstarch	25 mL
½	green bell pepper, cut into strips	½
½	red bell pepper, cut into strips	½

1. *Meatballs:* In a large bowl, combine ground beef, onion, garlic, egg, cracker crumbs, salt and pepper. Mix well. Form into 24 1-inch (2.5 cm) meatballs.

2. In a skillet, heat oil over medium heat. Brown meatballs, in batches, on all sides, for about 8 minutes, adding more oil as necessary. Remove from pan with slotted spoon and drain on paper towel.

3. *Sauce:* Meanwhile, in a medium saucepan over low heat, warm reserved pineapple juice, water, brown sugar, cider vinegar and soy sauce for 5 minutes or until sugar dissolves. Stir in cornstarch. Increase heat to medium-high. Bring to a boil and continue stirring until smooth.

4. Add meatballs, pineapple tidbits and green and red pepper strips. Cover and simmer over medium-low heat for 20 minutes or until vegetables are tender.

MAKE AHEAD
Form meatballs, cover and refrigerate for up to 1 day. Just before serving, cook meatballs and prepare sauce as directed.

Moroccan Meatballs

SERVES 4

This Moroccan-inspired dish is best served with couscous, especially the flavorful way I like to prepare it.

TIP

To add extra flavor to your couscous, use chicken stock in place of water (1¼ cups/300 mL liquid to 1 cup/250 mL instant couscous). Season stock with a pinch each of turmeric, ginger and cinnamon. Once the couscous is cooked, sprinkle generously with dried mint flakes, chopped fresh parsley and a handful of dried cranberries. If desired, also add ½ cup (125 mL) each sautéed onion and zucchini to couscous.

VARIATION

Use ground beef in place of ground lamb.

- ✦ Preheat oven to 350°F (180°C)
- ✦ Baking sheet, lightly sprayed

2 tsp	olive oil	10 mL
½	small onion, chopped	½
1	clove garlic, minced	1
1 lb	ground lamb	500 g
½ cup	couscous	125 mL
1	egg, beaten	1
2 tbsp	chopped fresh parsley	25 mL
½ tsp	turmeric	2 mL
¼ tsp	ground cinnamon	1 mL
¼ tsp	ground ginger	1 mL
	Couscous (see Tip, left)	

1. In a small nonstick skillet, heat oil over medium heat. Sauté onion and garlic for 3 minutes or until browned.

2. In a medium bowl, combine ground lamb, couscous, egg, parsley, turmeric, cinnamon and ginger. Add sautéed onion and garlic. Mix well.

3. Form into 20 1½-inch (4 cm) meatballs. Place on prepared baking sheet.

4. Bake in preheated oven for 30 minutes, turning after 15 minutes, until browned on all sides and no longer pink. Serve with couscous.

MAKE AHEAD

Prepare side dish of couscous and refrigerate for up to 2 days. Meatballs can be formed, covered and refrigerated for up to 1 day. Just before serving, cook meatballs as directed in Step 4.

Porcupines

SERVES 4

This easy meatball recipe is suited to a weekday dinner and pairs well with the rice or pasta of your choice. These meatballs are dubbed "porcupines" because the rice in the meat mixture vaguely resembles porcupine quills.

TIP
To reduce the number of dishes to wash, heat the sauce in a microwave-safe casserole in the microwave.

VARIATION
Use ground turkey in place of ground beef.

✦ Preheat oven to 350°F (180°C)
✦ 8-cup (2 L) casserole

MEATBALLS

1 lb	lean ground beef	500 g
½ cup	uncooked instant rice	125 mL
1 tbsp	dried onion flakes	15 mL
2	cloves garlic, minced	2
1	egg, beaten	1
½ tsp	salt	2 mL
¼ tsp	freshly ground black pepper	1 mL
2 tbsp	olive oil for frying (approx.)	25 mL

SAUCE

1	can (10 oz/284 mL) condensed tomato soup, undiluted	1
1 tbsp	Worcestershire sauce	15 mL
½ tsp	garlic powder	2 mL
2	drops hot pepper sauce	2

1. *Meatballs:* In a large bowl, combine ground beef, rice, onion flakes, garlic, egg, salt and pepper. Form into 24 1-inch (2.5 cm) meatballs.

2. In a skillet, heat oil over medium-high heat. Brown meatballs, in batches, turning several times to brown on all sides, for about 8 minutes, adding more oil as necessary. Remove from pan with slotted spoon and drain on paper towel.

3. *Sauce:* In a small saucepan, dilute tomato soup with an equal quantity of water. Stir in Worcestershire sauce, garlic powder and hot pepper sauce. Mix well. Bring to a boil over high heat, stirring constantly.

4. Place meatballs in casserole. Pour sauce over meatballs, stirring well to coat.

5. Bake in preheated oven for 30 minutes or until sauce is thickened.

MAKE AHEAD

Form meatballs, cover and refrigerate for up to 1 day. Just before serving, cook meatballs and prepare sauce as directed. Baked meatballs can also be frozen in sauce in an airtight container for up to 1 month. Let thaw. Reheat in microwave on High for 20 minutes, stirring partway through.

Swedish Meatballs

SERVES 4

These tasty, creamy meatballs are a pleasant change from the usual tomato-based meatballs. Serve with fettuccine.

TIP
Use a nonstick skillet to fry meatballs so you only need a little oil.

VARIATION
Use a combination of ground veal and ground beef.

MEATBALLS

1 lb	lean ground beef	500 g
½ cup	finely minced onion	125 mL
2	cloves garlic, minced	2
¼ cup	dry bread crumbs	50 mL
2 tbsp	milk	25 mL
2 tbsp	Worcestershire sauce	25 mL
1 tbsp	sweet relish	15 mL
1	egg, lightly beaten	1
½ tsp	salt	2 mL
¼ tsp	freshly ground black pepper	1 mL
2 tbsp	olive oil for frying (approx.)	25 mL

SAUCE

1	can (10 oz/284 mL) condensed cream of mushroom soup	1
⅔ cup	2% milk	150 mL
1 tbsp	chopped fresh dill	15 mL

1. *Meatballs:* In a large bowl, combine ground beef, onion, garlic, bread crumbs, milk, Worcestershire sauce, sweet relish, egg, salt and pepper. Form into 24 1-inch (2.5 cm) meatballs.

2. In a skillet, heat oil over medium heat. Brown meatballs, in batches, turning several times to brown on all sides, for about 8 minutes, adding more oil as necessary. Remove from pan with slotted spoon and drain on paper towel.

3. *Sauce:* Pour off fat from skillet. Return to medium heat and add mushroom soup, milk and dill. Stir until blended. Return meatballs to skillet. Cover and simmer, stirring occasionally, for 15 minutes or until sauce is thickened.

MAKE AHEAD
Form meatballs, cover and refrigerate for up to 1 day. Just before serving, cook meatballs and prepare sauce as directed.

Sweet-and-Sour Meatballs

SERVES 4

This traditional recipe for sweet-and-sour meatballs, a typical side dish served at Jewish holiday dinners, is fabulous over rice. It can easily be doubled.

TIPS

For a thicker sauce, remove lid and bake, uncovered, for final 10 minutes.

Meatballs are delicious served over hot white rice.

VARIATION

Use ground veal or a combination of ground veal and ground beef in place of ground beef.

✦ Preheat oven to 350°F (180°C)
✦ 8-cup (2 L) casserole

MEATBALLS

1 lb	lean ground beef	500 g
2 tbsp	minced onion	25 mL
1	clove garlic, minced	1
½ cup	dry bread crumbs	125 mL
1	egg, beaten	1
½ tsp	salt	2 mL
¼ tsp	freshly ground black pepper	1 mL
2 tbsp	olive oil for frying (approx.)	25 mL

SAUCE

¾ cup	pineapple juice	175 mL
½ cup	ketchup	125 mL
¼ cup	packed brown sugar	50 mL
2 tbsp	vinegar	25 mL
2 tbsp	freshly squeezed lemon juice	25 mL

1. *Meatballs:* In a large bowl, combine ground beef, onion, garlic, bread crumbs, egg, salt and pepper. Form into 24 1-inch (2.5 cm) meatballs.

2. In a skillet, heat oil over medium heat. Brown meatballs, in batches, turning several times to brown on all sides, for about 8 minutes, adding more oil as necessary. Remove from pan with slotted spoon and drain on paper towel.

3. *Sauce:* Meanwhile, in a medium saucepan over medium-high heat, bring pineapple juice, ketchup, brown sugar, vinegar and lemon juice to a boil. Reduce heat to low and simmer for 5 minutes or until well blended.

4. Place meatballs in casserole. Pour sauce over top. Cover and bake in preheated oven for 30 minutes or until sauce is thickened.

MAKE AHEAD

Prepare recipe as directed in a microwave-safe dish and freeze for up to 1 month. Let thaw. Reheat in microwave on High for 20 minutes, stirring partway through. Baked meatballs can also be frozen in sauce in an airtight container for up to 1 month. Let thaw. Reheat in microwave on High for 20 minutes, stirring partway through.

Mango Chicken Meatballs

SERVES 4

This marvelous mélange of fruity mango glaze and tamari-spiked meatballs is the ultimate in low-fat, high-flavor food. Serve over rehydrated rice stick noodles with steamed broccoli for a complete Asian-themed menu.

TIPS

To rehydrate rice stick noodles, soak in boiling water for 5 to 10 minutes or until softened. For this recipe, I prefer the thick rice noodles (about 8 oz/250 g).

Tamari is made with a higher proportion of soybeans than regular soy sauce and is rich in color and flavor. It is available at Asian supermarkets and other specialty food stores.

VARIATIONS

Replace marmalade with additional mango chutney.

Use regular soy sauce in place of tamari.

✦ Preheat oven to 375°F (190°C)
✦ Baking sheet, lightly sprayed

MEATBALLS

1 lb	lean ground chicken	500 g
2	cloves garlic, minced	2
1 tbsp	dried onion flakes	15 mL
1	egg, beaten	1
½ cup	uncooked instant rice	125 mL
¼ cup	tamari (see Tips, left)	50 mL

GLAZE

½ cup	apple jelly	125 mL
¼ cup	orange marmalade	50 mL
¼ cup	mango chutney	50 mL
	Juice of ½ lemon	

1. *Meatballs:* In a medium bowl, combine ground chicken, garlic, onion flakes, egg, instant rice and tamari. Mix well. Form into 24 1-inch (2.5 cm) meatballs.

2. Place meatballs on prepared baking sheet. Bake in preheated oven for 25 minutes, turning after 15 minutes, or until browned and no longer pink.

3. *Glaze:* Meanwhile, in a medium saucepan over medium-high heat, bring apple jelly, marmalade, mango chutney and lemon juice to a boil. Boil for 3 minutes or until thickened.

4. Add meatballs to saucepan, stirring well to coat. Cover saucepan. Boil gently, stirring occasionally, for 15 minutes or until glaze is thickened.

MAKE AHEAD

Freeze baked meatballs in glaze in an airtight container for up to 1 month. Let thaw. Reheat in microwave on High for 20 minutes, stirring partway through.

Turkey Meatballs

SERVES 4

These low-fat turkey meatballs, with their sweet, sticky sauce, are terrific served over rice.

TIP
The pinch of thyme in this recipe gives a very subtle thyme flavor. You can increase it to ¼ tsp (1 mL) for a stronger impact or omit it altogether, depending on your preference. Make sure your dried thyme is fresh for best results.

VARIATIONS
Use black currant jelly in place of grape jelly.

To add zing, add 1 to 2 tbsp (15 to 25 mL) prepared chili sauce to sauce.

✦ Preheat oven to 375°F (190°C)
✦ Baking sheet, lightly sprayed

MEATBALLS

1 lb	lean ground turkey	500 g
½ cup	fresh bread crumbs	125 mL
1	egg, beaten	1
¼ cup	finely minced shallots	50 mL
1	clove garlic, minced	1
2 tbsp	chopped fresh parsley	25 mL
½ tsp	salt	2 mL
¼ tsp	freshly ground black pepper	1 mL
⅛ tsp	dried thyme leaves (optional)	0.5 mL

SAUCE

1 cup	grape jelly	250 mL
⅓ cup	prepared mustard	75 mL

1. *Meatballs:* In a medium bowl, combine ground turkey, bread crumbs, egg, minced shallots, garlic, parsley, salt, pepper, and thyme, if using. Form into 24 1-inch (2.5 cm) meatballs.

2. Place meatballs on prepared baking sheet. Bake in preheated oven for 25 minutes, turning after 15 minutes, or until browned and no longer pink.

3. *Sauce:* Meanwhile, in a medium saucepan over medium-high heat, bring grape jelly and mustard to a boil, stirring constantly. Boil for 5 minutes or until jelly is melted.

4. Add meatballs. Reduce heat to low and simmer, covered, for 10 minutes or until thickened, stirring occasionally to coat.

MAKE AHEAD
Form meatballs, cover and refrigerate for up to 1 day. Just before serving, prepare sauce. Bake and simmer meatballs in sauce as directed. Baked meatballs can also be frozen in sauce in an airtight container for up to 1 month. Let thaw. Reheat in microwave on High for 20 minutes, stirring partway through.

Cocktail Meatballs

MAKES 42 MEATBALLS

These easy-to-make meatballs are suitable for serving to company as appetizers (don't forget the fancy toothpicks and the chafing dish) or for a main entrée when accompanied by rice and salad.

TIP

For an ideal presentation, serve meatballs in a shallow chafing dish, stirring sauce occasionally.

✦ Preheat oven to 375°F (190°C)
✦ Baking sheet, lightly sprayed

MEATBALLS

$\frac{1}{2}$ cup	fresh bread crumbs	125 mL
$\frac{1}{4}$ cup	milk	50 mL
1 lb	lean ground beef	500 g
$\frac{1}{4}$ cup	minced onion	50 mL
2	cloves garlic, minced	2
1	egg, beaten	1
$1\frac{1}{2}$ tbsp	chopped fresh parsley	22 mL
2 tsp	Worcestershire sauce	10 mL
$\frac{1}{4}$ tsp	salt	1 mL
$\frac{1}{4}$ tsp	freshly ground black pepper	1 mL

SAUCE

1	bottle (12 oz/341 mL) prepared chili sauce	1
1	jar (8 oz/250 mL) grape jelly	1

1. *Meatballs:* In a bowl, combine bread crumbs and milk. Soak for 2 minutes.

2. In a large bowl, combine ground beef, soaked bread crumbs, onion, garlic, egg, parsley, Worcestershire sauce, salt and pepper. Shape into 42 $\frac{1}{2}$-inch (2 cm) meatballs. Place on prepared baking sheet. Bake in preheated oven for 25 minutes, turning after 15 minutes, or until browned and no longer pink.

3. *Sauce:* In a medium saucepan, heat chili sauce and grape jelly over medium-high heat, stirring constantly, for 5 minutes or until jelly is melted.

4. Add meatballs to saucepan, stirring well to coat. Reduce heat to medium-low and simmer, covered, for 15 minutes or until sauce is thickened.

MAKE AHEAD

Form meatballs, cover and refrigerate for up to 1 day. Just before serving, bake meatballs and prepare sauce as directed. Baked meatballs can also be frozen in sauce in an airtight container for up to 1 month. Let thaw. Reheat in microwave on High for 20 minutes, stirring partway through.

Pasta

Chicken Broccoli Shells

SERVES 6

The attractive presentation of this creamy chicken and broccoli dish guarantees it will impress guests — or your deserving family.

TIP
Each box of large pasta shells contains 28 shells.

VARIATION
Use ground turkey in place of ground chicken.

✦ Preheat oven to 350°F (180°C)
✦ 12-cup (3 L) casserole, greased

1 tbsp	olive oil	15 mL
1	small onion, chopped	1
2	cloves garlic, minced	2
1 cup	finely chopped broccoli florets	250 mL
1 1/4 lbs	lean ground chicken	625 g
2/3 cup	white wine	150 mL
1 1/2 tsp	herbes de Provence (see Tip, page 50)	7 mL

CREAM SAUCE

3 tbsp	butter, divided	45 mL
1/4 cup	minced shallots	50 mL
1/2 cup	chopped mushrooms	125 mL
1 tbsp	all-purpose flour	15 mL
3/4 cup	half-and-half (10%) cream	175 mL
3/4 cup	milk	175 mL
1/2 tsp	dried basil leaves	2 mL
1/4 tsp	garlic powder	1 mL
	Salt and freshly ground black pepper, to taste	
1	box (8 oz/250 g) large pasta shells (see Tip, left)	1
	Freshly grated Parmesan cheese	

1. In a skillet, heat oil over medium heat. Sauté onion, garlic and broccoli for 5 minutes or until vegetables are softened.

2. Add ground chicken and cook, breaking up chicken, for 7 minutes longer or until no longer pink.

3. Add white wine and herbes de Provence. Reduce heat to medium-low and simmer, uncovered, stirring occasionally, for 10 minutes or until wine is reduced and sauce is thickened.

4. *Cream Sauce:* Meanwhile, in another saucepan, melt 1 tbsp (15 mL) of the butter over medium heat. Sauté shallots and mushrooms for 2 minutes. Stir in flour. Gradually whisk in cream and milk. Gradually add remaining butter, whisking constantly, until melted. Season with basil, garlic powder, salt and pepper.

5. Meanwhile, in a large saucepan of boiling salted water, cook pasta shells for 12 minutes or until al dente. Drain and let cool.

6. Stuff each shell with chicken broccoli mixture. Place shells in a single layer in bottom of prepared casserole. Pour Cream Sauce evenly over top. Bake in preheated oven for 20 minutes or until heated through.

7. Sprinkle shells with Parmesan cheese before serving.

MAKE AHEAD

Prepare shells in advance. Refrigerate or freeze until required. Prepare Cream Sauce before serving as directed in Step 4.

Chicken Sausage and Pasta Casserole

SERVES 4

The proliferation of new chicken and turkey sausage products opens up a wide range of culinary possibilities with markedly less fat than traditional pork sausages but just as much flavor.

TIPS

When simmering tomato sauces, keep the sauce from splattering on the stovetop with a splatter screen, available at kitchenware and department stores.

If opting for dried herbs, use 2 tsp (10 mL) each oregano and basil and 1 tsp (5 mL) dried parsley flakes.

To save cleanup time, let your ovenproof Dutch oven or saucepan do double duty as a casserole dish. After simmering sausage and vegetable medley in tomato sauce, add spaghetti to Dutch oven and bake as directed.

✦ Preheat oven to 375°F (190°C)
✦ 12-cup (3 L) casserole

2 tsp	olive oil	10 mL
1 lb	sun-dried tomato and herb chicken sausage (also known as chicken Mediterranean sausage), cut into chunks	500 g
1	onion, chopped	1
2	cloves garlic, minced	2
1	zucchini, sliced	1
1 cup	sliced mushrooms	250 mL
2	cans (each 14 oz/398 mL) tomato sauce	2
2 tbsp	chopped fresh oregano	25 mL
2 tbsp	chopped fresh basil	25 mL
1 tbsp	chopped fresh parsley	15 mL
	Salt and freshly ground black pepper, to taste	
2 cups	broken spaghetti (uncooked)	500 mL
1 cup	water	250 mL
½ cup	freshly grated Parmesan cheese	125 mL

1. In a Dutch oven or large saucepan, heat oil over medium-high heat. Sauté sausage, onion and garlic for 7 minutes or until sausage is browned on outside and no longer pink inside.

2. Add zucchini and mushrooms and sauté for 2 minutes longer.

VARIATIONS
Use any flavored turkey
or chicken sausage.

This tasty casserole can
also be prepared with
rigatoni or another
favorite pasta in place
of spaghetti. Larger
pasta will require up to
15 minutes additional
baking time.

3. Add tomato sauce, oregano, basil, parsley, salt and pepper. Bring to a boil. Reduce heat to medium-low and simmer, uncovered or with a splatter screen (see Tips, far left), for 15 minutes or until thickened.

4. Add pasta and water to tomato sauce. Mix well. Pour into casserole. Sprinkle with Parmesan cheese. Bake in preheated oven for 45 minutes, stirring partway, or until bubbling and pasta is al dente.

Chorizo Sausage and Pasta Bake

SERVES 4 TO 6

Here's an easy yet hearty pasta bake that is intensely flavored and teeming with vegetables. By broiling, rather than frying, the sausage, much of the fat drips off, but the spicy chorizo sausage essence remains.

TIP
If you prefer not to serve this casserole-style, omit Steps 5 and 6. Simply serve the pasta topped with the sausage and tomato sauce. Sprinkle each serving with mozzarella cheese.

VARIATION
Use a different variety of sausage, such as Italian.

✦ Preheat oven to 350°F (180°C)
✦ Broiler pan with rack
✦ 12-cup (3 L) casserole

1 lb	soft chorizo sausage	500 g
12 oz	rigatini (small-ridged tubes) or any tubular pasta such as penne	375 g
1 tbsp	olive oil	15 mL
1	small onion, chopped	1
1	clove garlic, minced	1
½	red bell pepper, cut into chunks	½
½	yellow bell pepper, cut into chunks	½
1	zucchini, sliced	1
2	cans (each 14 oz/398 mL) tomato sauce	2
1 tsp	dried Italian seasoning	5 mL
½ tsp	salt	2 mL
½ tsp	granulated sugar	2 mL
¼ tsp	freshly ground black pepper	1 mL
¼ tsp	dried marjoram leaves	1 mL
¼ cup	chopped fresh parsley	50 mL
2 cups	shredded mozzarella cheese (about 8 oz/250 g), divided	500 mL

1. Place sausage on rack on broiler pan. Bake in preheated oven for 30 minutes, turning every 10 minutes, or until no longer pink. Slice into large chunks.

2. Meanwhile, in a large saucepan of boiling salted water, cook rigatini for 8 to 10 minutes or until al dente. Drain and let cool.

3. In a large saucepan, heat oil over medium heat. Sauté onion and garlic for 3 minutes or until onions are softened. Add red and yellow peppers and sauté for 2 minutes longer. Add zucchini and sauté for 1 minute.

Seven-Layer Dinner (page 91)

4. Pour in tomato sauce. Season with Italian seasoning, salt, sugar, pepper and marjoram. Stir in parsley. Add sausage pieces. Reduce heat to medium-low and simmer for 15 minutes or until thickened.

5. In bottom of casserole, layer half of the pasta, then half of the sauce. Sprinkle with 1 cup (250 mL) of the cheese. Repeat layers.

6. Bake in preheated oven, uncovered, for 30 minutes or until cheese is melted and casserole is bubbling.

MAKE AHEAD
Prepare sausage, vegetable and tomato sauce up to 2 days in advance. Cover and refrigerate until needed. Freeze the sauce for up to 1 month.

Wild Rice Chicken Loaf
(page 110)

Classic Lasagna

SERVES 8

This superb lasagna recipe gets top marks for both taste and presentation. I like to spend a Sunday baking it, then serve half that night and freeze the other half for a later date.

TIP

If time allows, simmer the ground beef and tomato sauce for 30 minutes for better flavor.

VARIATION

Use ricotta cheese in place of dry cottage cheese.

+ Preheat oven to 350°F (180°C)
+ 13-by 9-inch (3 L) glass baking dish
+ Deep skillet

2 tbsp	olive oil	25 mL
1	onion, chopped	1
2	cloves garlic, minced	2
1 lb	lean ground beef	500 g
½ tsp	salt	2 mL
¼ tsp	freshly ground black pepper	1 mL
1	can (14 oz/398 mL) tomato sauce, divided	1
1	can (28 oz/796 mL) crushed tomatoes	1
1	can (5½ oz/156 mL) tomato paste	1
½ cup	dry red wine	125 mL
1 tbsp	granulated sugar	15 mL
1 tbsp	Worcestershire sauce	15 mL
1 tsp	dried oregano leaves	5 mL
1 tsp	dried basil leaves	5 mL
2	drops hot pepper sauce	2
12	lasagna noodles	12
1½ lbs	dry cottage cheese, divided	750 g
4 cups	shredded mozzarella cheese (about 1 lb/500 g), divided	1 L
1 cup	freshly grated Parmesan cheese, divided	250 mL
½ cup	sliced mushrooms	125 mL
½	green bell pepper, sliced into strips	½

1. In a deep skillet, heat oil over medium heat. Sauté onion and garlic for 3 minutes or until softened.

2. Add ground beef. Season with salt and pepper. Brown beef, breaking up meat, for 7 minutes or until no longer pink.

3. Set aside $\frac{1}{3}$ cup (75 mL) of the tomato sauce. Add remaining tomato sauce to skillet along with canned tomatoes, tomato paste and red wine. Season with sugar, Worcestershire sauce, oregano, basil and hot pepper sauce. Reduce heat to medium-low and simmer, covered, stirring occasionally, for 20 minutes or until thickened.

4. Meanwhile, in a large saucepan of boiling salted water, cook lasagna noodles for 8 to 10 minutes or until al dente. Drain and let cool.

5. Spread reserved tomato sauce in bottom of baking dish. Place one-third of the lasagna noodles over top. Pour one-third of the sauce over noodles. Layer with one-third of the cottage cheese, one-third of the mozzarella and one-third of the Parmesan. Repeat layers twice. Sprinkle mushroom slices and green pepper slices over top.

6. Bake in preheated oven for 60 minutes or until bubbling vigorously. Let cool for 10 minutes before serving.

MAKE AHEAD

Lasagna freezes well for up to 1 month. Be sure to freeze it in an airtight container or wrap well with a layer of plastic wrap, then foil.

Lazy Lasagna

This fab but fast dish packs all the flavor of lasagna without all the fuss. Serve with garlic bread and salad.

TIP
Use pre-shredded mozzarella and Parmesan to speed things up.

VARIATION
Use another favorite store-bought pasta sauce or your own homemade tomato sauce.

◆ Preheat oven to 350°F (180°C)
◆ 11-by 7-inch (2 L) glass baking dish, lightly greased

1 tbsp	olive oil	15 mL
½	onion, chopped	½
2	cloves garlic, minced	2
1 lb	lean ground beef	500 g
1	jar (26 oz/700 mL) red wine and herb pasta sauce (see Variation, left)	1
6 oz	broad egg noodles	175 g
1½ cups	shredded mozzarella cheese (about 6 oz/175 g)	375 mL
¼ cup	sour cream	50 mL
1 cup	1% cottage cheese	250 mL
¾ cup	freshly grated Parmesan cheese	175 mL

1. In a medium saucepan, heat oil over medium heat. Sauté onion and garlic for 3 minutes or until softened.

2. Add ground beef and brown, stirring frequently, for 7 minutes or until no longer pink. Stir in pasta sauce. Bring to a boil. Reduce heat to medium-low and simmer for 15 minutes or until thickened.

3. Meanwhile, in a large pot of boiling salted water, cook egg noodles for 8 minutes or until al dente. Drain and let cool.

4. In a medium bowl, combine mozzarella, sour cream and cottage cheese.

5. Place half of the noodles in bottom of prepared baking dish. Spread the cheese mixture over top. Layer with half of the meat mixture, the remaining noodles and then the remaining meat mixture. Top with freshly grated Parmesan. Bake, uncovered, in preheated oven for 35 minutes or until bubbling.

Sausage and Ricotta Cheese Lasagna

SERVES 8

Spicy sausage and creamy ricotta cheese complement each other in this lasagna. A few shortcuts, such as using stewed tomatoes and tomato sauce with Italian spices, jazz up this rendition.

TIP
If you prefer, use plain tomato sauce and season with 1 tsp (5 mL) each dried basil and oregano leaves instead of tomato sauce with Italian spices.

VARIATION
Use Italian sausage or another favorite sausage.

✦ Preheat oven to 375°F (190°C)
✦ 13-by 9-inch (3 L) glass baking dish

1 tbsp	olive oil	15 mL
1	onion, chopped	1
3	cloves garlic, minced	3
½	red bell pepper, chopped	½
½	green bell pepper, chopped	½
1 lb	soft chorizo sausage, casings removed	500 g
1	can (28 oz/796 mL) stewed tomatoes	1
1	can (28 oz/796 mL) tomato sauce with Italian spices (see Tip, left)	1
1 cup	dry red wine	250 mL
1 tbsp	balsamic vinegar	15 mL
12	lasagna noodles	12
1 lb	ricotta cheese, divided	500 g
2 cups	shredded mozzarella cheese (about 8 oz/250 g), divided	500 mL
¾ cup	freshly grated Parmesan cheese, divided	175 mL

1. In a large saucepan or deep skillet, heat oil over medium heat. Sauté onion and garlic for 3 minutes or until softened.

2. Add red and green peppers and sauté for 2 minutes longer. Add sausage meat and cook for 7 minutes or until no longer pink.

3. Add stewed tomatoes, tomato sauce, red wine and balsamic vinegar. Bring to a boil, stirring occasionally. Reduce heat to medium-low and simmer for 20 minutes or until sauce is thickened.

4. Meanwhile, in a large saucepan of boiling salted water, cook lasagna noodles for 8 to 10 minutes or until al dente. Drain and let cool.

5. Spread ½ cup (125 mL) of the sausage tomato sauce in bottom of baking dish. Arrange a layer of noodles to fit bottom. Spread with one-third of remaining sauce. Top with one-third of the ricotta, one-third of the mozzarella and one-third of the Parmesan. Repeat layers twice. Bake in preheated oven for 30 minutes or until bubbling.

Pastitsio

SERVES 6

This delectable Greek dish is perfect to serve to company or to make ahead on the weekend for midweek dining. However, the simmering spiced beef imparts such a lovely aroma, you may not be able to resist digging in right away!

TIP

Give yourself a couple of hours to whip up this recipe. With the various components, pastitsio is a little on the labor-intensive side, but like most good food it's well worth the effort.

VARIATION

Use ground lamb in place of ground beef.

✦ Preheat oven to 375°F (190°C)
✦ 13-by 9-inch (3 L) glass baking dish

1 tbsp	olive oil	15 mL
1	onion, chopped	1
3	cloves garlic, minced	3
1 lb	lean ground beef	500 g
1	can (14 oz/398 mL) stewed tomatoes (about 1½ cups/375 mL)	1
½ cup	dry red wine	125 mL
2 tbsp	tomato paste	25 mL
¼ tsp	ground cloves	1 mL
½ tsp	ground cinnamon	2 mL
½ tsp	salt	2 mL
⅛ tsp	ground nutmeg	0.5 mL
Pinch	freshly ground black pepper	Pinch
½ cup	chopped fresh parsley	125 mL
2 cups	elbow macaroni (8 oz/250 g)	500 mL

CHEESY CUSTARD

2 tbsp	butter	25 mL
¼ cup	all-purpose flour	50 mL
2 cups	warm milk	500 mL
1	egg, beaten	1
1 cup	freshly grated Parmesan cheese, divided	250 mL
Pinch	each salt, freshly ground black pepper and nutmeg	Pinch

1. In a large skillet, heat oil over medium heat. Sauté onion and garlic for 3 minutes or until softened.

2. Brown ground beef, stirring frequently and breaking up meat, for 7 minutes or until no longer pink. Drain off any excess fat.

3. Add stewed tomatoes, wine, tomato paste, cloves, cinnamon, salt, nutmeg and pepper. Reduce heat to medium-low and simmer, uncovered, for 25 minutes or until thickened. Add parsley and simmer for 5 minutes longer.

4. Meanwhile, in a large saucepan of boiling salted water, cook macaroni for 8 minutes or until al dente. Drain and set aside.

5. *Cheesy Custard:* In a saucepan, melt butter over medium heat. Stir in flour and cook, stirring, for 1 minute. Gradually pour in warm milk, whisking constantly until blended. Add beaten egg and $2/3$ cup (150 mL) of the Parmesan cheese. Continue stirring for 3 minutes or until sauce is thickened. Season with salt, pepper and nutmeg.

6. Mix 1 cup (250 mL) of the Cheesy Custard sauce with macaroni. Spread in bottom of baking dish. Top with beef mixture. Spread remaining sauce over top. Sprinkle with remaining Parmesan cheese. Bake in preheated oven for 35 minutes or until bubbling and top is browned.

MAKE AHEAD

Prepare meat sauce up to 1 day in advance. Reheat before assembling pastitsio.

Sausage and Ricotta Manicotti Shells

Serve up stuffed shells to friends at your own dinner party or take along this dish to a potluck. Stuffed shells can be prepared in advance and reheated at your party location.

TIP

I've used freshly grated Parmesan here, which takes the filling up a notch.

VARIATION

Use a milder Italian sausage or another variety of sausage.

✦ Preheat oven to 375°F (190°C)
✦ Shallow casserole, lightly sprayed

1 lb	hot Italian sausage, casings removed	500 g
2	cloves garlic, minced	2
½ cup	chopped leeks	125 mL
½ cup	chopped zucchini	125 mL
21	manicotti shells (14 shells per 8 oz/250 g box)	21
1 lb	ricotta cheese	500 g
½ cup	freshly grated Parmesan cheese, divided	125 mL
¼ cup	chopped fresh parsley	50 mL
1 tsp	dried basil leaves	5 mL
½ tsp	salt	2 mL
¼ tsp	freshly ground black pepper	1 mL
1	can (19 oz/540 mL) pasta sauce	1
1 cup	shredded mozzarella cheese	250 mL

1. In a saucepan over medium heat, cook sausage for 7 minutes or until no longer pink.

2. Add garlic, leeks and zucchini. Cook for 3 minutes longer or until leeks start to brown. Set aside.

3. Meanwhile, in a large saucepan of boiling salted water, cook manicotti shells for 12 minutes or until al dente. Drain and let cool.

4. In a large bowl, combine ricotta, ¼ cup (50 mL) of the Parmesan, parsley, basil, salt and pepper. Add sausage mixture and mix well.

5. Fill each manicotti shell with about ¼ cup (50 mL) of filling. Arrange in a single layer in prepared casserole. Top with pasta sauce. Sprinkle with mozzarella and remaining Parmesan cheese.

6. Bake in preheated oven for 35 minutes or until cooked through and bubbling.

Sausage and Rigatoni

SERVES 4

Sausage and pasta is an excellent combination, especially in this simple yet satisfying dish.

TIP
Vegetable bouillon cubes are now available alongside chicken and beef bouillon cubes. They are very flavorful and add to the tang of this dish.

VARIATIONS
Use chicken stock in place of vegetable stock.

Use a favorite sausage other than Italian.

8 oz	hot Italian sausage, sliced into chunks	250 g
1 tsp	olive oil (optional)	5 mL
1	green onion, chopped	1
2	cloves garlic, minced	2
½	red bell pepper, cut into chunks	½
½	green bell pepper, cut into chunks	½
8 oz	fresh pea pods	250 g
1 cup	vegetable stock (see Tip, left)	250 mL
2 tsp	Dijon mustard	10 mL
1 tsp	dried oregano leaves	5 mL
¼ cup	chopped fresh parsley	50 mL
8 oz	rigatoni or penne pasta	250 g
1 cup	shredded mozzarella cheese	250 mL

1. In a nonstick skillet over medium heat, cook sausage chunks for 7 minutes or until no longer pink.

2. Add olive oil, if necessary to prevent sticking, green onion, garlic and red and green peppers. Sauté for 3 minutes. Add pea pods and sauté for 2 minutes longer or until pea pods are tender.

3. In a bowl, combine vegetable stock, Dijon mustard and oregano. Pour into skillet. Add parsley, mixing well. Reduce heat to medium-low and simmer for 2 minutes longer.

4. Meanwhile, in a large saucepan of boiling salted water, cook rigatoni for 8 to 10 minutes or until al dente. Drain and let cool.

5. Serve pasta topped with sausage and vegetable sauce. Sprinkle mozzarella cheese on individual servings.

MAKE AHEAD
Complete up to the end of Step 4. Combine pasta, sausage and vegetable sauce in 12-cup (3 L) casserole. Stir in mozzarella, mixing well to coat pasta. Cover and refrigerate for up to 2 days. To reheat, bake in preheated 350°F (180°C) oven for 30 minutes or until heated through.

Turkey Orzo Casserole

SERVES 4 TO 6

*Orzo is united with
ground turkey and
french-fried onions in
this delicious and colorful
dinner that no one will
ever guess is so easy
to make.*

TIPS

Orzo is rice-shaped
pasta. Look for it
alongside other pasta
at the supermarket.

French-fried onions
are usually found
in the canned
vegetable section
in the supermarket.

VARIATION

Top casserole with corn
flakes crumbs in place
of french-fried onions.

✦ Preheat oven to 375°F (190°C)
✦ 10-cup (2.5 L) casserole

1 tbsp	olive oil (approx.)	15 mL
¼ cup	chopped red onion	50 mL
2	cloves garlic, minced	2
½	red bell pepper, chopped	½
1 lb	lean ground turkey	500 g
2 cups	broccoli florets	500 mL
1	stalk celery, chopped	1
1 cup	orzo (see Tips, left)	250 mL
1	can (10 oz/284 mL) condensed cream of mushroom soup, undiluted	1
1 cup	shredded mozzarella cheese, divided	250 mL
1	can (3 oz/79 g) french-fried onions (see Tips, left)	1

1. In a skillet, heat oil over medium heat. Sauté onion, garlic and red pepper for 5 minutes or until vegetables are softened.

2. Add ground turkey and cook, breaking up turkey, for 7 minutes or until no longer pink.

3. Remove turkey and vegetables with slotted spoon and place in casserole.

4. In same skillet, heat additional oil if necessary and sauté broccoli and celery for 3 minutes or until softened. Add to casserole.

5. Meanwhile, in a saucepan of boiling salted water, cook orzo for 6 to 8 minutes or until al dente. Drain. Add to casserole and mix well. Stir in cream of mushroom soup and half of the mozzarella cheese.

6. Top casserole with remaining mozzarella and french-fried onions. Bake in preheated oven for 30 minutes or until hot and bubbling.

MAKE AHEAD

This recipe can be prepared up to Step 5 up to 1 day in advance and refrigerated until serving. Add french-fried onions and the remaining shredded cheese just before baking.

Turkey, Wild Mushroom and Basil Spaghetti Sauce

SERVES 4

This quick, light dinner is a cinch to create on a busy weeknight. You'll have most of the ingredients on hand, but if not, improvise! Use button mushrooms instead of wild mushrooms, dried basil leaves instead of fresh, and Parmesan from a shaker instead of freshly grated. Serve with a salad for a complete dinner.

TIP
Look for cremini (brown) mushrooms instead of white button mushrooms for a more intense flavor. Shiitake mushrooms are my preferred wild mushroom because of their earthiness. Today's "wild" mushrooms, widely available in supermarket produce sections, are not really wild given that they are cultivated. A more accurate name nowadays for shiitake, oyster and portobello is "exotic" mushrooms.

VARIATION
Use ground beef in place of ground turkey.

1 tbsp	olive oil	15 mL
1	onion, chopped	1
2	cloves garlic, minced	2
2 cups	sliced wild and button mushroom mixture (see Tip, left)	500 mL
½	green bell pepper, chopped	½
½	red bell pepper, chopped	½
1 lb	lean ground turkey	500 g
2	cans (each 19 oz/540 mL) spicy pasta sauce	2
2 tbsp	chopped fresh basil	25 mL
¼ cup	chopped fresh parsley	50 mL
½ tsp	salt	2 mL
¼ tsp	freshly ground black pepper	1 mL
8 oz	spaghetti	250 g
	Freshly grated Parmesan cheese (optional)	

1. In a medium saucepan, heat oil over medium heat. Sauté onion, garlic and mushrooms for 5 minutes or until vegetables are softened.

2. Add green and red peppers and ground turkey and sauté, breaking up turkey, for 7 minutes or until no longer pink.

3. Add pasta sauce, basil, parsley, salt and pepper. Bring to a boil. Reduce heat to medium-low and simmer, uncovered, for 20 minutes or until thickened.

4. Meanwhile, in a large saucepan of boiling salted water, cook spaghetti for 8 to 10 minutes or until al dente. Drain.

5. Top each serving of spaghetti with sauce. Sprinkle with Parmesan cheese, if using.

MAKE AHEAD
Prepare sauce in advance. Refrigerate for up to 3 days or freeze for up to 1 month.

Veal Florentine Shells

Stuffed shells offer a fabulous presentation along with great texture and taste. They look beautiful on a serving platter decorated with sprigs of fresh parsley and lemon slices.

VARIATION
Use ground beef in place of ground veal.

◆ Preheat oven to 375°F (190°C)
◆ 12-cup (3 L) shallow casserole

1 tbsp	olive oil	15 mL
2	cloves garlic, minced	2
1	shallot, minced	1
1 cup	chopped mushrooms	250 mL
1 lb	ground veal	500 g
1	package (10 oz/300 g) fresh spinach, steamed and cooled	1
¾ cup	beef stock	175 mL
½ cup	white wine	125 mL
1 tsp	dried oregano leaves	5 mL
½ tsp	dried thyme leaves	2 mL
1	small bay leaf	1
½ cup	chopped fresh parsley	125 mL
8 oz	large pasta shells (about 28 shells)	250 g
3 cups	homemade or store-bought pasta sauce	750 mL
	Freshly grated Parmesan cheese	

1. In a skillet, heat oil over medium heat. Sauté garlic, shallot and mushrooms for 5 minutes or until vegetables are softened.

2. Add ground veal and cook, breaking up meat, for 7 minutes or until no longer pink.

3. Squeeze excess liquid from spinach. Add to skillet along with beef stock, wine, oregano, thyme and bay leaf. Reduce heat to medium-low and simmer, uncovered, for 15 minutes or until liquid is reduced and flavors are blended. Remove bay leaf. Stir in parsley.

4. Meanwhile, in a large saucepan of boiling salted water, cook pasta shells for 8 to 12 minutes or until al dente. Drain and let cool.

5. Fill each shell with 1½ tbsp (22 mL) of the meat and spinach mixture. Arrange in a single layer in bottom of casserole.

6. Top with pasta sauce. Sprinkle with Parmesan cheese. Bake in preheated oven for 30 minutes or until bubbling.

MAKE AHEAD

Prepare shells in advance. Refrigerate for up to 3 days. Complete up to the end of Step 5 and freeze in an airtight container for up to 1 month. Let thaw. Top with pasta sauce and bake in preheated 350°F (180°C) oven for 30 to 40 minutes or until heated through.

Weeknight Spaghetti and Meat Sauce

SERVES 4

In the same amount of time it takes to order a pizza, you can whip up this comfort food supper. Serve with salad and garlic toast. Enlist older children to make the salad.

TIP

In a hurry? Replace canned tomato sauce and all the seasonings with a jar or can of seasoned pasta sauce. Let simmer for 10 to 15 minutes to allow flavors to blend.

VARIATION

Use ground chicken in place of ground beef.

1 tbsp	olive oil	15 mL
1	onion, chopped	1
2	cloves garlic, minced	2
½	green bell pepper, chopped	½
½	red bell pepper, chopped	½
½ cup	sliced mushrooms (optional)	125 mL
1 lb	lean ground beef	500 g
	Salt and freshly ground black pepper, to taste	
2	cans (each 14 oz/398 mL) tomato sauce (see Tip, left)	2
1 tsp	dried oregano leaves	5 mL
1 tsp	granulated sugar	5 mL
½ tsp	Worcestershire sauce	2 mL
¼ tsp	hot pepper flakes	1 mL
1	bay leaf	1
8 oz	spaghetti	250 g
	Freshly grated Parmesan cheese	

1. In a saucepan, heat oil over medium heat. Sauté onion, garlic and green and red peppers for 5 minutes or until vegetables are softened. Add mushrooms, if using, and sauté for 2 minutes longer.

2. Add ground beef and brown, stirring constantly and breaking up meat, for 7 minutes or until no longer pink. Drain off excess fat. Season with salt and pepper.

3. Add tomato sauce, oregano, sugar, Worcestershire sauce, hot pepper flakes and bay leaf. Bring to a boil over medium-high heat. Reduce heat to medium-low and simmer, stirring occasionally, for 20 minutes or until thickened. Cover saucepan with splatter screen (see Tips, page 126).

4. Meanwhile, in a large saucepan of boiling salted water, cook spaghetti for 8 to 10 minutes or until al dente. Drain and set aside.

5. Remove bay leaf. Top spaghetti with meat sauce. Sprinkle with freshly grated Parmesan cheese.

MAKE AHEAD
Double the ingredients for the meat sauce and freeze half in a microwave-safe container for up to 1 month. Thaw in microwave for a speedy suppertime solution.

Spaghetti and Meatballs

SERVES 4

Certain comfort foods never go out of style. My sons are never disappointed with a platter of spaghetti and meatballs and a tossed salad on the side.

TIP
Sugar reduces some of the acidity of the crushed tomatoes.

VARIATION
Add ½ cup (125 mL) dry red wine to tomato sauce. Simmer as directed.

✦ Preheat oven to 375°F (190°C)
✦ Baking sheet, lightly greased

MEATBALLS

1 lb	lean ground beef	500 g
¼ cup	dry bread crumbs	50 mL
1	egg, beaten	1
2	cloves garlic, minced	2
2 tbsp	finely minced onion	25 mL
1 tsp	dried basil leaves	5 mL
1 tsp	dried oregano leaves	5 mL
½ tsp	salt	2 mL
¼ tsp	freshly ground black pepper	1 mL

SAUCE

1 tbsp	olive oil	15 mL
1	small onion, minced	1
2	cloves garlic, minced	2
1	can (28 oz/796 mL) crushed tomatoes	1
1½ tsp	dried Italian seasoning	7 mL
1 tsp	granulated sugar	5 mL
½ tsp	dried parsley flakes	2 mL
½ tsp	hot pepper flakes	2 mL
1 lb	spaghetti	500 g
	Freshly grated Parmesan cheese (optional)	

1. *Meatballs:* In a medium bowl, combine ground beef, bread crumbs, egg, garlic, onion, basil, oregano, salt and pepper. Form into 24 1-inch (2.5 cm) meatballs. Place on prepared baking sheet. Bake in preheated oven for 25 minutes, turning after 15 minutes, or until browned outside and no longer pink inside.

2. *Sauce:* Meanwhile, in a Dutch oven or large saucepan, heat oil over medium heat. Sauté onion and garlic for 3 minutes or until softened. Add crushed tomatoes, Italian seasoning, sugar, parsley flakes and hot pepper flakes. Increase heat to medium-high and bring to a boil. Reduce heat to medium-low and simmer for 20 minutes.

3. Add baked meatballs to tomato sauce. Stir to coat. Simmer, covered, for 25 minutes or until thickened.

4. Meanwhile, in a large saucepan of boiling salted water, cook spaghetti for 8 to 10 minutes or until al dente. Drain.

5. Serve meatballs and sauce over spaghetti. Sprinkle with Parmesan cheese, if using.

MAKE AHEAD

Baked meatballs can be cooled and frozen in a single layer on a baking sheet. Once frozen, transfer to a resealable plastic bag and freeze for up to 1 month. Thaw in refrigerator before adding to tomato sauce.

Ground Beef Goulash
a.k.a. American Chop Suey

SERVES 4

When I was growing up in the 1960s, everybody's mother had her own macaroni and ground beef dish. This is an ideal quick, weeknight meal when hockey practices or swimming lessons make it impossible for a leisurely dinner.

TIP

Feel free to throw in red or green peppers or other vegetables from your crisper.

VARIATION

Use mozzarella cheese in place of Cheddar or omit cheese altogether.

+ Preheat oven to 350°F (180°C)
+ 10-cup (2.5 L) casserole

1 tbsp	olive oil	15 mL
1	small onion, chopped	1
2	cloves garlic, minced	2
½ cup	diced celery	125 mL
1 lb	lean ground beef	500 g
	Salt and freshly ground black pepper, to taste	
2	cans (each 19 oz/540 mL) stewed tomatoes, including juice	2
¼ cup	chopped fresh parsley	50 mL
2 cups	elbow macaroni	500 mL
½ cup	frozen corn kernels	125 mL
1 cup	shredded Cheddar cheese	250 mL

1. In a medium saucepan, heat oil over medium heat. Sauté onion, garlic and celery for 5 minutes or until softened.

2. Brown ground beef, stirring frequently and breaking up meat, for 7 minutes or until no longer pink. Season with salt and pepper.

3. Add stewed tomatoes with juice and fresh parsley. Stir well, breaking up tomatoes. Bring to a boil. Reduce heat to low and simmer for 15 minutes or until thickened.

4. Meanwhile, in a saucepan of boiling salted water, cook macaroni for 8 minutes or until al dente. Drain well and add to saucepan. Stir to combine.

5. Pour macaroni and beef mixture into casserole. Mix in corn. Sprinkle Cheddar cheese over top. Bake in preheated oven for 30 minutes or until bubbling.

Skillet Suppers

Three-Cheese Penne Hamburger Skillet

SERVES 4

Think outside the box for this homemade version of those pricey packaged hamburger noodle dinners. After trying this one, you'll wonder why you ever banked on boxed dinners in the first place!

TIPS

Processed cheese block is essential for the right creamy consistency.

The broth and processed cheese are quite salty, so additional salt is omitted from the ingredient list.

VARIATION

Use rotini or other tube pasta in place of penne.

◆ Electric skillet or deep skillet

1 tbsp	olive oil	15 mL
1	small onion, chopped	1
2	cloves garlic, minced	2
½	green bell pepper, chopped	½
1 lb	lean ground beef	500 g
1 tbsp	Worcestershire sauce	15 mL
1 tbsp	Dijon mustard	15 mL
	Freshly ground black pepper, to taste	
2½ cups	beef stock	625 mL
2 cups	penne	500 mL
1 cup	processed cheese block, such as Velveeta, cubed (4 oz/125 g) (see Tip, left)	250 mL
¾ cup	Monterey Jack cheese, cubed or shredded (3 oz/90 g)	175 mL
¾ cup	Cheddar cheese, cubed or shredded (3 oz/90 g)	175 mL

1. In an electric skillet, heat oil over medium heat. Sauté onion, garlic and green pepper for 5 minutes or until vegetables are softened.

2. Add ground beef and brown, breaking up meat, for 7 minutes or until no longer pink. Add Worcestershire sauce and Dijon mustard. Stir well. Season with pepper.

3. Add stock and penne. Mix well. Increase heat to medium-high and bring to a boil. Cover and boil, stirring occasionally, for 8 to 10 minutes or until noodles are tender.

4. Reduce heat to medium-low. Add processed, Monterey Jack and Cheddar cheeses. Stir well for 3 minutes or until cheeses are melted. Serve immediately.

Salisbury Steak

SERVES 4

This traditional dish is a nice change from regular hamburgers. The gravy and fried onions are a must!

TIP
Serve with mashed potatoes and Brussels sprouts or vegetable of your choice.

VARIATION
Omit the mushrooms. Use homemade gravy.

3 tbsp	vegetable oil, divided	45 mL
1	small onion, finely minced	1
1½ lbs	lean ground sirloin	750 g
1	egg	1
1 tbsp	Worcestershire sauce	15 mL
½ tsp	salt	2 mL
½ tsp	garlic powder	2 mL
¼ tsp	dry mustard	1 mL
¼ tsp	freshly ground black pepper	1 mL
1	onion, sliced	1
1 cup	sliced mushrooms	250 mL
1	package (1 oz/25 g) brown gravy (yield 1 cup/250 mL)	1

1. In a skillet, heat 1 tbsp (15 mL) of the oil over medium-low heat. Sauté minced onion for 3 minutes or until browned.

2. Place ground sirloin in a large bowl. Add cooked onions, egg, Worcestershire sauce, salt, garlic powder, mustard and pepper. Shape into 6 small patties, about ¾-inch (2 cm) thick. Score with knife.

3. In a skillet, heat remaining oil over medium heat. Cook Salisbury steaks for 10 to 12 minutes, turning every 2 to 3 minutes, or until cooked through. Transfer to a plate and keep warm. Add sliced onion and mushrooms to skillet and sauté for 6 minutes or until browned.

4. Meanwhile, prepare gravy according to package instructions. Stir into mushroom mixture.

5. Serve Salisbury steaks topped with mushroom and onion gravy.

MAKE AHEAD
Prepare steaks up to 1 day in advance. Before serving, prepare onions, mushrooms and gravy. Top steaks with mushroom and onion gravy and reheat in 350°F (180°C) oven for 20 minutes or until heated through.

Pantry Chow Mein

SERVES 4

This is a great answer to a weekday "What do I make for dinner tonight?" quandary. You should have most of the ingredients on hand, but if not, be creative — that's what chow mein is all about.

TIP
Feel free to add other vegetables, such as peppers, broccoli or cabbage, to the stir-fry. Serve with crunchy chow mein noodles as well, if desired.

VARIATION
Use ground chicken or turkey in place of ground beef.

✦ Wok or deep skillet

2 tbsp	vegetable oil, divided	25 mL
½	onion, chopped	½
2	cloves garlic, minced	2
1 tbsp	minced fresh gingerroot	15 mL
1 lb	lean ground beef	500 g
¾ cup	sliced carrots	175 mL
¾ cup	sliced celery	175 mL
¼ cup	soy sauce, divided	50 mL
3 tbsp	hoisin sauce	45 mL
1 tbsp	sherry	15 mL
1	can (10 oz/284 mL) mushrooms, drained and liquid reserved	1
1	can (8 oz/250 mL) bamboo shoots, drained	1
1 lb	precooked chow mein noodles (broad or thin)	500 g
1 tbsp	cornstarch	15 mL
½ cup	frozen peas	125 mL

1. In a wok, heat 1 tbsp (15 mL) of the oil over medium-high heat. Sauté onion, garlic and ginger for 3 minutes or until onions start to brown.

2. Reduce heat to medium. Add ground beef, carrots and celery. Sauté, breaking up meat, for 7 minutes or until no longer pink.

3. Combine 2 tbsp (25 mL) of the soy sauce, hoisin sauce and sherry. Pour over beef mixture, stirring well. Add mushrooms and bamboo shoots. Sauté for 2 minutes longer.

4. Remove beef mixture from wok. Add remaining oil. Add noodles and cook, stirring constantly, for 2 minutes.

5. Pour reserved liquid from canned mushrooms (about $2/3$ cup/150 mL) into microwave-safe glass measuring cup. Stir in remaining soy sauce and cornstarch. Microwave on High for 1 minute, stirring partway through, until cornstarch is dissolved. Mix well. Pour over noodles. Sauté for 3 minutes longer.

6. Return beef mixture to wok over low heat and mix well with vegetables and noodles. Add frozen peas. Warm mixture for 5 minutes longer to allow flavors to combine, stirring frequently.

Ground Lamb Curry

SERVES 4

Coconut milk and lemongrass complement each other in this unconventional ground meat dish. You'll be pleasantly surprised at how well suited ground meat is to a curry.

TIP

If you can't find lemongrass, use a 2-inch (5 cm) strip of lemon zest, minced.

VARIATION

Use ground beef in place of ground lamb.

✦ 2 skillets

2 tsp	olive oil	10 mL
1	onion, chopped	1
2	cloves garlic, minced	2
1 tbsp	minced fresh gingerroot	15 mL
½ cup	coconut milk	125 mL
¼ cup	tamarind paste (see Tips, page 156)	50 mL
1 tbsp	curry powder	15 mL
¼ tsp	hot pepper flakes	1 mL
1	stalk lemongrass, chopped (see Tip, left)	1
1 lb	ground lamb	500 g
	Salt and freshly ground black pepper, to taste	
	Cooked basmati rice	
	Fresh cilantro (optional)	

1. In a skillet, heat oil over medium heat. Sauté onion, garlic and ginger for 3 minutes or until onions are softened. Add coconut milk, tamarind paste, curry powder, hot pepper flakes and lemongrass. Increase heat to medium-high and bring to a boil. Reduce heat to low and simmer, uncovered, for 5 minutes or until coconut milk is heated through.

2. Meanwhile, in another skillet over medium heat, brown lamb, breaking up meat, for 7 minutes or until no longer pink. Season with salt and pepper. When cooked through, drain fat.

3. Pour sauce from first skillet over ground lamb. Simmer for 30 minutes, stirring occasionally, or until flavors have blended and sauce is bubbling. Add water if necessary to prevent sticking.

4. Serve over basmati rice. Garnish with cilantro, if desired.

Ground Veal à la Parmigiana

SERVES 4

This ground veal recipe delivers a more economical version of the beloved veal Parmesan.

TIP
Spicy pasta sauce works well in this dish.

✦ Preheat oven to 350°F (180°C)
✦ 8-cup (2 L) shallow casserole

½ cup	dry bread crumbs	125 mL
1 tbsp	freshly grated Parmesan cheese	15 mL
½ tsp	garlic powder	2 mL
½ tsp	dried oregano leaves	2 mL
	Salt and freshly ground black pepper, to taste	
1 lb	lean ground veal	500 g
¼ cup	all-purpose flour	50 mL
2	eggs, beaten	2
2 tbsp	olive oil	25 mL
1 cup	tomato-based pasta sauce	250 mL
1 cup	shredded mozzarella cheese	250 mL
¼ cup	freshly grated Parmesan cheese	50 mL

1. In a shallow bowl, combine bread crumbs, 1 tbsp (15 mL) Parmesan cheese, garlic powder, oregano, salt and pepper.

2. Divide veal into 4 portions. Shape each portion into a flat ½-inch (1 cm) thick cutlet.

3. Place flour and beaten egg in separate shallow bowls. Dip each cutlet into egg, then flour, then egg again and then bread crumb mixture. Refrigerate for 15 minutes to firm up.

4. In a skillet, heat oil over medium heat. Brown veal for 4 minutes per side or until golden brown.

5. Place in shallow casserole. Pour tomato sauce over veal "cutlets." Sprinkle with mozzarella, then Parmesan. Bake in preheated oven for 20 minutes or until veal is no longer pink, sauce is bubbling and cheese is melted.

Spanish Rice Italian-Style

SERVES 4 AS AN ENTRÉE,
6 TO 8 AS A SIDE DISH

This dish does double-duty as an elegant entrée or as a side dish with some depth.

TIP
Instead of an electric skillet, use a stovetop skillet with a lid. Be sure to keep the temperature low.

VARIATION
Use ground beef in place of ground veal.

◆ Electric skillet or large skillet with lid

2 tbsp	olive oil	25 mL
1 cup	uncooked long-grain white rice	250 mL
1	small onion, chopped	1
2	cloves garlic, minced	2
½	green bell pepper, diced	½
½	red bell pepper, diced	½
1 lb	lean ground veal	500 g
1	can (28 oz/796 mL) stewed tomatoes, including juice	1
1 cup	water (approx.)	250 mL
½ tsp	hot pepper flakes	2 mL
½ tsp	dried Italian seasoning	2 mL
	Salt and freshly ground black pepper, to taste	
¼ cup	chopped fresh parsley	50 mL
	Freshly grated Parmesan cheese	

1. In an electric skillet or stovetop skillet (see Tip, left), heat oil over medium heat. Add rice and cook, stirring constantly, for 5 minutes or until slightly browned.

2. Add onion, garlic, green and red peppers and ground veal. Cook, stirring and breaking up meat, for 7 minutes or until veal is no longer pink and onion is softened and starting to brown.

3. Add stewed tomatoes with juice, water, hot pepper flakes, Italian seasoning, salt and pepper. Increase heat to medium-high and bring to a boil. Reduce heat to low. Cover and simmer for 20 minutes or until rice is tender. Check occasionally to ensure there is sufficient liquid, adding additional water if necessary. At the end of cooking time, most of the liquid should be absorbed.

4. Sprinkle each serving with parsley and Parmesan cheese.

Southwest Mess

SERVES 4

This Southwest-inspired tangy skillet supper can be prepared easily and quickly.

TIPS

Serve with shredded Monterey Jack and Cheddar cheese, sour cream, sliced black olives and tortilla chips.

Vegetable cocktail adds punch to this recipe.

VARIATION

Use ground beef in place of ground pork.

✦ Electric skillet or large skillet with lid

2 tbsp	olive oil	25 mL
½	onion, chopped	½
1	clove garlic, minced	1
1 lb	lean ground pork	500 g
½ tsp	salt	2 mL
¼ tsp	freshly ground black pepper	1 mL
	Green hot pepper sauce, to taste	
½	green bell pepper, chopped	½
½	red bell pepper, chopped	½
1½ cups	uncooked long-grain white rice	375 mL
1 tbsp	chili powder	15 mL
¼ tsp	cumin seeds	1 mL
2 cups	tomato-based vegetable cocktail (see Tips, left)	500 mL
2 cups	water (approx.)	500 mL
1	can (14 oz/398 mL) red kidney beans, drained and rinsed	1
1	can (12 oz/341 mL) corn kernels, drained	1

1. In an electric skillet or stovetop skillet (see Tip, page 154), heat oil over medium heat. Sauté onion and garlic for 3 minutes or until browned.

2. Add ground pork. Season with salt, pepper and green hot pepper sauce. Increase heat to high. Brown, breaking up meat, for 7 minutes or until no longer pink.

3. Add green and red peppers. Sauté for 1 minute. Add rice, chili powder and cumin seeds. Sauté, stirring constantly, for 1 to 2 minutes.

4. Pour in vegetable cocktail, water and kidney beans. Stir well. Increase heat to medium-high. Bring to a boil. Add corn.

5. Reduce heat to low. Cover skillet tightly and simmer, stirring occasionally, for 20 minutes or until rice is tender. Check occasionally to ensure there is sufficient liquid, adding additional water if necessary.

Thai Pork and Noodles

SERVES 4

Thai fans will love this quick noodle dish. I paired it with thick Japanese udon noodles for Asian fusion.

TIP

Tamarind paste or concentrate is derived from the tamarind fruit after its seeds and fibers have been strained out. Tamarind, known for its acidic flavor, shows up in dishes across the Asian continent. Look for tamarind, usually dried, pickled in brine or puréed into paste, in Asian grocery stores.

VARIATIONS

Use additional hot curry paste, if desired, or add a minced hot pepper to the skillet before adding ground pork.

If desired, use reconstituted rice stick noodles in place of udon noodles.

½ cup	coconut milk	125 mL
¼ cup	tamarind paste (see Tips, left)	50 mL
2	stalks lemongrass, chopped	2
2	green onions, chopped	2
1 tsp	Thai green curry paste	5 mL
1 lb	lean ground pork	500 g
¼ cup	chopped fresh basil	50 mL
¼ cup	chopped fresh cilantro	50 mL
1 lb	udon noodles	500 g

1. In a skillet over medium-high heat, bring coconut milk, tamarind paste, lemongrass, green onions and curry paste to a boil.

2. Reduce heat to medium. Add ground pork and brown, breaking up meat, for 7 minutes or until no longer pink.

3. Add basil and cilantro. Reduce heat to low and simmer for 15 minutes to allow flavors to blend.

4. Meanwhile, in a saucepan of boiling salted water, cook udon noodles for 3 to 5 minutes. Drain.

5. In a large serving dish, combine cooked udon noodles and ground pork mixture. Mix well and serve.

Asian Chicken and Noodles

SERVES 4

The fragrant sauce gives the ground chicken, vegetables and noodles a boost in this dinner in a bowl. On any given day, most of us will have the bulk of the necessary ingredients on hand — or make it work with what's in your cupboard or fridge.

TIP
Vermicelli noodles are like very thin spaghetti, so they take less time to cook.

VARIATION
Use ground turkey in place of ground chicken.

✦ Wok (preferably nonstick) with lid

1 tbsp	vegetable oil	15 mL
2	green onions, chopped	2
1 tbsp	minced fresh gingerroot	15 mL
2	cloves garlic, minced	2
2 cups	cauliflower florets	500 mL
½	green bell pepper, chopped	½
½	red bell pepper, chopped	½
1 lb	lean ground chicken	500 g
8 oz	vermicelli noodles (see Tip, left)	250 g

SAUCE

⅓ cup	tamari (approx.)	75 mL
1 tbsp	seasoned rice vinegar	15 mL
4 tsp	sesame oil	20 mL
1 tsp	garlic chili sauce	5 mL
1 tsp	grated lime zest	5 mL
1½ tbsp	freshly squeezed lime juice	22 mL
1 tsp	packed brown sugar (optional)	5 mL
6 cups	shredded baby bok choy	1.5 L

1. In a wok, heat oil over medium-high heat. Sauté green onions, ginger, garlic, cauliflower florets and green and red peppers for 1 minute.

2. Add ground chicken and brown, breaking up chicken, for 5 minutes or until no longer pink.

3. Meanwhile, in a saucepan of boiling salted water, cook noodles for 6 to 7 minutes or until al dente. Drain and rinse.

4. *Sauce:* In a bowl, combine tamari, rice vinegar, sesame oil, garlic chili sauce, lime zest and juice and brown sugar, if using. Pour into wok. Stir well until blended.

5. Add bok choy. Stir well. Cover and cook for 2 minutes or until bok choy is tender. Add noodles and stir into vegetables and meat. Add additional tamari, if desired.

MAKE AHEAD
This dish can be prepared earlier in the day or the night before serving. Cover and refrigerate in a microwave-safe casserole for easy reheating. Reheat in microwave on High, stirring partway through, for 10 minutes or until heated through.

Turkey Stroganoff

SERVES 4

This lighthearted version of stroganoff offers another speedy supper solution with a respectable representation from all four major food groups.

TIP
Rinse noodles under cold water and drain well to prevent them from sticking together.

VARIATION
Use ground beef or ground chicken in place of ground turkey.

✦ Electric skillet or large skillet with lid

1 tbsp	olive oil	15 mL
1	shallot, minced	1
1 lb	lean ground turkey	500 g
¼ tsp	dried thyme leaves	1 mL
	Salt and freshly ground black pepper, to taste	
½	green bell pepper, chopped	½
2 cups	sliced mushrooms	500 mL
1	can (13.5 oz/385 mL) 2% evaporated milk	1
1 tsp	dry mustard	5 mL
2 tbsp	chopped fresh dill	25 mL
2 tbsp	chopped fresh parsley	25 mL
8 oz	medium egg noodles	250 g
1 cup	light sour cream	250 mL

1. In an electric skillet or large stovetop skillet (see Tip, page 154), heat oil over medium heat. Sauté shallot for 2 minutes.

2. Add ground turkey and brown, breaking up turkey, for 7 minutes or until no longer pink. Season with thyme, salt and pepper. Add green pepper and mushrooms. Sauté for 2 minutes.

3. Stir together evaporated milk and dry mustard. Slowly pour over ground turkey and vegetables. Add dill and parsley. Bring to a boil. Simmer, stirring often, for 3 minutes or until vegetables are tender.

4. Meanwhile, in a large saucepan of boiling salted water, cook egg noodles for 8 minutes or until al dente. Drain and rinse.

5. Gradually add noodles to skillet, stirring into ground turkey mixture. Stir in sour cream and heat through, stirring constantly. (Do not bring to a boil.)

Hamburger, Vegetable and Noodle Skillet

SERVES 6 TO 8

This recipe is a family standard. Whenever I have bits and pieces of various vegetables in my refrigerator, I know exactly what to make for dinner!

TIP

This makes a great "planned over" recipe, as opposed to "left over". (I like to purposely make extra in order to have leftovers.) Once cooked, it keeps well, covered, in the refrigerator for up to 3 days. Reheat in microwave. I like to use my deep-dish electric fry pan since it can easily hold all of the ingredients.

VARIATION

Add sliced mushrooms, zucchini or cabbage as desired at the same time as the celery, carrots, broccoli and cauliflower.

2 tsp	olive oil	10 mL
1	onion, chopped	1
2	cloves garlic, minced	2
½	red bell pepper, sliced into chunks	½
½	green bell pepper, sliced into chunks	½
1½ lbs	lean ground beef	750 g
¼ tsp	salt	1 mL
¼ tsp	freshly ground black pepper	1 mL
2 tbsp	prepared chili sauce	25 mL
1	stalk celery, sliced	1
2	carrots, peeled and sliced	2
1 to 2 cups	broccoli florets	250 to 500 mL
1 to 2 cups	cauliflower florets	250 to 500 mL
1	can (10 oz/284 mL) condensed cream of mushroom soup, undiluted	1
2 cups	wide egg noodles (about 4 oz/125 g)	500 mL
2 cups	water (approx.)	500 mL

1. In a large nonstick skillet, heat oil over medium heat. Sauté onion, garlic and red and green peppers for 5 minutes or until vegetables are softened.

2. Add ground beef and brown, breaking up meat, for 7 minutes or until no longer pink. Add salt and pepper. Stir in chili sauce.

3. Add celery, carrots, broccoli and cauliflower. Sauté for 3 minutes. Stir in cream of mushroom soup. Mix well.

4. Add egg noodles and water. Mix well, ensuring noodles are completely covered.

5. Increase heat to medium-high. Cover skillet and bring to a boil, stirring occasionally. Reduce heat to medium-low and boil gently for 20 minutes, stirring occasionally, or until noodles and vegetables are tender. Add additional water if necessary to keep moist.

Spiced Ground Lamb in Pita

SERVES 4

This fragrant dish is best served in pita pockets. In place of pita, serve over couscous or rice.

TIP

Warm pita pockets in toaster oven at 350°F (180°C) for 5 to 8 minutes, turning once. Serve lamb in warmed pita halves.

VARIATION

Use ground beef in place of ground lamb.

1 tsp	olive oil	5 mL
1	onion, chopped	1
3	cloves garlic, minced	3
1 tsp	ground cumin	5 mL
¼ tsp	ground cinnamon	1 mL
⅛ tsp	ground cloves	0.5 mL
⅛ tsp	ground cardamom	0.5 mL
1 lb	ground lamb	500 g
1 cup	tomato sauce	250 mL
4	pitas, sliced in half (see Tip, left)	4

1. In a nonstick skillet, heat oil over medium heat. Sauté onion and garlic for 3 minutes or until softened. Stir in cumin, cinnamon, cloves and cardamom. Mix well until combined.

2. Add ground lamb and brown, breaking up meat, for 7 minutes or until no longer pink.

3. Drain off excess fat. Add tomato sauce. Increase heat to medium-high. Bring to a boil.

4. Reduce heat to medium-low and simmer for 20 minutes, stirring occasionally, or until thickened. Serve in pita halves.

Classic Lasagna (page 130)

Savory Pies

Asian Chicken and Noodles (page 157)

Shepherd's Pie

SERVES 4 TO 6

This classic ground beef dish, said to have originated in England as a great use for Sunday dinner's leftover mashed potatoes and roast beef, is frequently requested by my sons. Somehow, though, I never seem to have leftover mashed potatoes, so I'm always starting from scratch!

TIP

In place of fresh steamed carrots, use ¾ cup (175 mL) frozen carrots. You can also use 2 cups (500 mL) mixed frozen peas, carrots and corn.

VARIATION

Use ketchup in place of prepared chili sauce.

✦ Preheat oven to 375°F (190°C)
✦ 12-cup (3 L) casserole

1 tsp	vegetable oil	5 mL
1	onion, chopped	1
1	clove garlic, minced	1
1½ lbs	lean ground beef	750 g
2	carrots, peeled and sliced (see Tip, left)	2
¾ cup	frozen peas	175 mL
¾ cup	frozen corn kernels	175 mL
½ cup	ketchup	125 mL
2 tbsp	prepared chili sauce	25 mL
1 tbsp	Worcestershire sauce	15 mL
	Salt and freshly ground black pepper, to taste	
8	medium potatoes, peeled and cut	8
¼ cup	warm milk	50 mL
1 tbsp	butter	15 mL
1 tbsp	freshly grated Parmesan cheese	15 mL

1. In a large nonstick skillet, heat oil over medium heat. Sauté onion and garlic for 3 minutes or until softened.

2. Add ground beef and brown, stirring frequently and breaking up meat, for 7 minutes or until no longer pink. Drain off excess fat.

3. Meanwhile, in a microwave-safe dish, combine carrots and 2 tbsp (25 mL) water. Microwave on High for 5 minutes. (Or steam carrots in water in saucepan on stovetop just until tender.) Add carrots, peas and corn to ground beef mixture.

4. Stir in ketchup, chili sauce and Worcestershire sauce. Season with salt and pepper and mix well. Simmer for 10 minutes longer to allow flavors to blend.

5. Meanwhile, in a saucepan of boiling salted water, cook potatoes for 15 minutes or until tender. Drain and mash. Mash in milk and butter. Season with salt and pepper.

6. Spoon ground beef and vegetable mixture into bottom of casserole. Spread mashed potatoes evenly on top. Sprinkle with Parmesan cheese. Bake in preheated oven for 35 minutes or until hot and bubbling. Broil for 5 minutes longer or until potatoes start to brown. Serve immediately.

MAKE AHEAD
When making mashed potatoes for another meal, plan on cooking extra for this dish.

Spinach and Beef Strudel

This gorgeous pie is definitely a crowd-pleaser. Serve it at a lunch or dinner party and the compliments are sure to come your way.

TIP

This recipe requires about one-third to half a box of phyllo sheets. Reserve remainder for another use.

◆ Preheat oven to 350°F (180°C)
◆ 13-by 9-inch (3 L) metal baking pan

BEEF MIXTURE

1 tbsp	olive oil	15 mL
1	onion, chopped	1
2	cloves garlic, minced	2
1	jalapeño pepper, seeded and minced	1
1 lb	lean ground beef	500 g
1/2	red bell pepper, chopped	1/2
1/2	green bell pepper, chopped	1/2
1 cup	sliced mushrooms	250 mL

SPINACH MIXTURE

1	package (10 oz/300 g) frozen spinach, thawed and chopped	1
1 lb	ricotta cheese	500 g
1/4 cup	crumbled feta cheese	50 mL
2 tbsp	freshly grated Parmesan cheese	25 mL
1 tsp	dried onion flakes	5 mL
1/2 tsp	ground nutmeg	2 mL
	Freshly ground black pepper, to taste	

STRUDEL

8	sheets phyllo pastry	8
	Olive oil	
1/2 cup	fresh bread crumbs, divided	125 mL
1/4 cup	freshly grated Parmesan cheese, divided	50 mL

1. *Beef Mixture:* In a skillet, heat oil over medium heat. Sauté onion for 2 minutes or until softened. Add garlic and jalapeño and sauté for 2 minutes longer.

2. Add ground beef, red and green peppers and mushrooms. Cook over medium heat, stirring and breaking up meat, for 7 minutes or until peppers are tender and ground beef is no longer pink.

3. *Spinach Mixture:* Meanwhile, squeeze excess liquid from spinach. In a large bowl, combine spinach, ricotta cheese, feta cheese, Parmesan cheese and dried onion flakes. Sprinkle with nutmeg and pepper. Set aside.

4. *Strudel:* Unfold phyllo sheets, covering stack with clean damp tea towel. Remove two sheets at a time and brush each with oil. Repeat four times to create a stack of eight sheets. Cut phyllo stack in half.

5. Place half of the stack on bottom of baking pan. (Cover remaining phyllo sheets with clean damp tea towel to prevent drying out.) Working quickly, sprinkle half of the bread crumbs and half of the Parmesan on top.

6. Spread spinach/ricotta mixture on phyllo pastry. Cover with beef mixture, spreading evenly.

7. Top with remaining phyllo pastry. Brush with oil. Sprinkle with remaining bread crumbs and remaining Parmesan. Bake in preheated oven for 40 minutes or until top is golden brown. Cut into squares and use a pie lifter to serve.

MAKE AHEAD

If you plan to prepare this ahead of time, bake for only 30 minutes and refrigerate, covered, for up to 2 days. To reheat, bake in preheated 350°F (180°C) oven for 20 minutes or until heated through.

Veal and Potato Pie

SERVES 4

Reminiscent of a shepherd's pie, this delicate version boasts a mild veal flavor enhanced by white wine.

TIP
For a fluffier texture, gently warm the milk in the microwave before adding to mashed potatoes.

VARIATION
Use ground turkey in place of ground veal.

+ Preheat oven to 375°F (190°C)
+ 12-cup (3 L) casserole, greased

1 tbsp	olive oil	15 mL
1	onion, chopped	1
2	cloves garlic, minced	2
1 lb	lean ground veal	500 g
1/4 tsp	dried thyme leaves	1 mL
	Salt and freshly ground black pepper, to taste	
1 cup	canned stewed tomatoes	250 mL
1/2 cup	dry white wine	125 mL
2 tbsp	tomato paste	25 mL
2 tsp	Worcestershire sauce	10 mL
1 tsp	granulated sugar	5 mL
1/2 tsp	dried oregano leaves	2 mL
1	bay leaf	1
6	medium potatoes, peeled and quartered	6
1/4 cup	warm milk	50 mL
1 tbsp	butter	15 mL
1/4 cup	freshly grated Parmesan cheese	50 mL

1. In a saucepan, heat oil over medium heat. Sauté onion and garlic for 3 minutes or until onion is softened.

2. Add ground veal and cook, breaking up meat, for 7 minutes or until no longer pink. Season with thyme, salt and pepper.

3. Add stewed tomatoes, wine, tomato paste, Worcestershire sauce, sugar, oregano and bay leaf. Simmer, uncovered, for 20 minutes or until thickened. Remove bay leaf.

4. Meanwhile, in a saucepan of boiling salted water, cook potatoes for 15 minutes or until tender. Drain and mash with milk, butter, salt and pepper.

5. Spoon half of the mashed potatoes into bottom of prepared casserole. Spread veal mixture over top. Top with remaining mashed potatoes. Sprinkle with Parmesan. Bake in preheated oven for 30 minutes or until hot and bubbling.

MAKE AHEAD
Prepare mashed potatoes in advance or use leftover mashed potatoes.

Taco Pie

This savory pie will get top marks from your family. Give the dish even more kick by using hot salsa. If you want it less spicy, reduce the amount of chili powder and use a mild taco sauce.

VARIATION
Bake without the cheese. Add cheese to taco pie along with lettuce and tomato.

◆ Preheat oven to 450°F (230°C)
◆ Baking sheet

1	9-inch (23 cm) frozen pie shell	1
1 tsp	vegetable oil	5 mL
1	small onion, chopped	1
2	cloves garlic, minced	2
1 lb	lean ground beef	500 g
1	can (10 oz/284 mL) condensed tomato soup, undiluted	1
1½ tbsp	chili powder	22 mL
½ tsp	ground cumin	2 mL
	Salt and freshly ground pepper, to taste	
½ cup	medium salsa	125 mL
1 tbsp	cornstarch	15 mL
½ cup	shredded Cheddar cheese	125 mL
½ cup	shredded mozzarella cheese	125 mL
1 cup	shredded lettuce	250 mL
1	tomato, diced	1
¼ cup	sliced black olives (optional)	50 mL
	Sour cream	

1. Place frozen pie shell on a baking sheet. Bake in preheated oven for 10 to 12 minutes or until golden brown. Reduce temperature to 350°F (180°C).

2. Meanwhile, in a nonstick skillet, heat oil over medium heat. Sauté onion and garlic for 3 minutes or until softened.

3. Add ground beef and brown, breaking up meat, for 7 minutes or until no longer pink. Drain off excess fat. Stir in tomato soup, chili powder and cumin. Season with salt and pepper.

4. In a small bowl, combine salsa and cornstarch, mixing well. Stir into skillet. Cook, stirring often, for 5 minutes or until bubbling and thickened.

5. Pour mixture into pie shell. Top with Cheddar and mozzarella cheeses. Bake for 15 minutes or until cheese is melted and top is golden brown.

6. Slice into pie wedges. Sprinkle each with lettuce, tomato and black olives, if using. Serve with sour cream.

Calzones

MAKES 10 CALZONES

These stuffed pizzas lend themselves to creativity. Include your family's favorite ingredients. Just make sure your selected fillings do not contain too much moisture or your dough will turn soggy.

VARIATION
Use hot Italian sausage in place of pepperoni. Sauté crumbled sausage (casings removed) after vegetables are softened for 7 minutes or until cooked through.

✦ Preheat oven to 425°F (220°C), with rack in lower third
✦ Baking stone or baking sheet, floured

1 tsp	olive oil	5 mL
½	onion, chopped	½
2	cloves garlic, minced	2
½	green bell pepper, chopped	½
½ cup	sliced mushrooms	125 mL
8 oz	smoked pepperoni sausage, sliced	250 g
½ cup	pizza sauce	125 mL
2 cups	shredded mozzarella cheese	500 mL
½ cup	ricotta cheese	125 mL
1 tsp	dried oregano leaves	5 mL
1 tsp	dried basil leaves	5 mL
	Salt and freshly ground pepper, to taste	
1	batch Pizza Bun Dough (see recipe, page 171)	1
	All-purpose flour	

1. In a nonstick skillet, heat oil over medium heat. Sauté onion, garlic, green pepper and mushrooms for 5 minutes or until softened.

2. Add pepperoni slices. Sauté for 1 minute. Add pizza sauce. Increase heat to medium-high and bring to a boil. Boil for 2 minutes or until thickened. Let cool slightly.

3. Meanwhile, in a medium bowl, combine mozzarella and ricotta cheeses. Mix in oregano, basil, salt and pepper. Add pepperoni and vegetable mixture. Mix well.

4. Divide dough into 10 pieces. Roll out each piece into a 6-inch (15 cm) circle. Place ⅓ cup (75 mL) of the filling on one side of circle, leaving a 1-inch (2.5 cm) border. Fold the other side of circle over the filling to form a half moon. Press edges of dough together and seal with fork dipped in flour. Repeat with remaining dough circles and filling.

5. Cut two slits on top of each calzone for steam to escape. Place on baking stone or floured baking sheet. Bake in preheated oven for 15 to 18 minutes or until golden brown.

MAKE AHEAD

Dough can be prepared in advance, wrapped in plastic wrap and frozen for up to 1 month. Let thaw overnight at room temperature. Once thawed, use immediately or refrigerate until required.

Pizza Buns

SERVES 8

These pizza buns would be "awesome" to serve at a kids' party or to bring to a potluck where pizza-loving children will be present. My 13-year-old son, Jesse, thinks this recipe is great. This versatile dough is also ideal for calzones.

TIP

On warm days, the dough will not need to rise a second time. Use dental floss or thread to neatly slice the roll into individual pizza buns.

VARIATION

Use spicy pasta sauce and omit the hot pepper sauce.

◆ Preheat oven to 425°F (220°C)
◆ 12-inch (30 cm) pizza pan

1 tsp	olive oil	5 mL
1	small onion, minced	1
2	cloves garlic, minced	2
12 oz	lean ground beef	375 g
1½ tsp	dried Italian seasoning	7 mL
	Salt and freshly ground black pepper, to taste	
¾ cup	tomato sauce	175 mL
½ tsp	hot pepper sauce	2 mL
1 cup	finely shredded mozzarella cheese	250 mL
1	batch Pizza Bun Dough (see recipe, page 171)	1
¼ cup	freshly grated Parmesan cheese	50 mL

1. In a nonstick skillet, heat oil over medium heat. Sauté onion and garlic for 3 minutes or until onions are softened.

2. Add ground beef and brown, breaking up meat, for 7 minutes or until no longer pink. Season with Italian seasoning, salt and pepper.

3. Stir in tomato sauce. Add hot pepper sauce. Reduce heat to medium-low and simmer for 5 minutes or until most of the liquid is evaporated. Remove from heat and stir in mozzarella cheese. Let cool slightly.

4. On lightly floured surface, roll out dough to 16-by 12-inch (40 by 30 cm) rectangle.

5. Spread beef mixture evenly over dough, leaving a 1-inch (2.5 cm) border along two long edges of dough. Moisten border with water. Starting at one long end, roll up tightly, jelly roll style. Pinch seams to seal.

6. Slice into 1-inch (2.5 cm) pieces (about 16) with sharp knife. Place pieces, cut side up and touching on pizza pan. Sprinkle each with Parmesan cheese. Let rise for 15 to 20 minutes longer.

7. Bake in preheated oven for 18 to 20 minutes or until crust is golden.

MAKE AHEAD
Prepare filling and refrigerate, covered, for up to 1 day.

Pizza Bun Dough

**MAKES ENOUGH FOR 16 PIZZA BUNS
OR 10 CALZONES**

2½ cups	all-purpose flour, divided (approx.)	625 mL
⅓ cup	whole wheat flour	75 mL
3 tbsp	granulated sugar	45 mL
1½ tsp	quick-rise (instant) yeast	7 mL
½ tsp	salt	2 mL
1 cup plus 2 tbsp	warm water	275 mL
1	egg, beaten	1
1 tbsp	vegetable oil	15 mL

1. In a small bowl, combine 1 cup (250 mL) of the all-purpose flour, whole wheat flour, sugar, yeast and salt. Stir in water. Mix well.

2. Add beaten egg and oil. Stir well to combine. Add remaining 1½ cups (375 mL) flour. Mix well.

3. On a lightly floured surface, knead dough for 5 to 10 minutes or until smooth and no longer sticky, adding more flour, up to 1 tbsp (15 mL) at a time, if dough is too sticky. Transfer to glass bowl. Cover with a clean tea towel and let rise in a warm place for approximately 1 hour or until doubled in size.

Easy Shepherd's Pie

SERVES 4

When you want the comfort of shepherd's pie but don't have the time, this recipe is a no-fuss winner.

TIP
Use salt sparingly when seasoning meat mixture since the soup mix and instant mashed potatoes are already salted.

✦ Preheat oven to 375°F (190°C)
✦ 8-cup (2 L) casserole

1 tsp	vegetable oil	5 mL
1	small onion, chopped	1
2	cloves garlic, minced	2
¼	green bell pepper, chopped	¼
1 lb	lean ground beef	500 g
	Freshly ground black pepper, to taste	
1 cup	mixed frozen peas, corn and carrots	250 mL
1½ cups	boiling water	375 mL
1	pouch (1.3 oz/39 g) beef noodle soup mix	1
1	box (215 g/7.5 oz) instant mashed potatoes	1
Pinch	paprika	Pinch

1. In a nonstick skillet, heat oil over medium heat. Sauté onion, garlic and green pepper for 5 minutes or until softened.

2. Add ground beef and brown, breaking up meat, for 7 minutes or until no longer pink.

3. Stir in frozen vegetables. Stir in water and soup mix. Reduce heat to medium-low and simmer for 10 minutes or until vegetables are softened. Season with pepper.

4. Meanwhile, prepare instant mashed potatoes according to package instructions.

5. Transfer beef mixture to casserole. Top with mashed potatoes. Sprinkle with paprika. Bake in preheated oven for 15 minutes or until heated through.

English Pork Pie

SERVES 4

This meat pie is a British specialty that shows up across England in pubs and corner bakeries. It is a meaty pie much loved across the pond for its flaky crust and mild flavor.

✦ Preheat oven to 425°F (220°C), with rack in lower third
✦ 9-inch (23 cm) pie plate or 2 5-inch (12.5 cm) pie plates, lightly greased

1 tsp	vegetable oil	5 mL
1 lb	lean ground pork	500 g
2 tbsp	beef stock	25 mL
1 tsp	dried sage leaves	5 mL
½ tsp	salt	2 mL
¼ tsp	freshly ground black pepper	1 mL
	Pastry for double-crust 9-inch (23 cm) pie (see recipe, page 175)	
1	egg, beaten	1

JELLY

½ cup	beef stock	125 mL
½ tsp	gelatine	2 mL

1. In a skillet, heat oil over medium heat. Add ground pork, beef stock, sage, salt and pepper. Brown, breaking up meat, for 7 minutes or until no longer pink.

2. Roll out half of the pastry and fit into pie plate. Pack in filling.

3. Roll out remaining pastry for top crust. Dampen edges of bottom and top crusts. Place top crust over pie and press seams to seal. Trim off any extra pastry.

4. Flute edges of pie. Brush pie with beaten egg. Cut a slit in the center to allow steam to escape. Bake in preheated oven for 30 minutes or until golden brown. Check after 20 minutes and rotate if baking unevenly.

5. *Jelly:* Meanwhile, in a small saucepan over low heat, stir together beef stock and gelatine and heat for 3 minutes or until dissolved and starting to thicken. Let cool slightly.

6. When pie is baked, pour jelly into pie through a funnel inserted in a hole in the top crust. Serve immediately.

Tourtière

SERVES 4 TO 6

This French Canadian meat pie is traditionally served on Christmas Eve. It can easily be baked ahead and frozen, ready to serve for a special occasion.

✦ Preheat oven to 425°F (220°C), with rack in lower third
✦ 9-inch (23 cm) pie plate, lightly greased

1	large potato, peeled and cut into chunks	1
1 lb	lean ground pork	500 g
8 oz	lean ground beef	250 g
2	cloves garlic, minced	2
1	onion, chopped	1
1 tsp	dried thyme leaves	5 mL
1 tsp	salt	5 mL
½ tsp	freshly ground black pepper	2 mL
½ tsp	dried sage leaves	2 mL
½ tsp	ground cloves	2 mL
	Pastry for double-crust 9-inch (23 cm) pie (see recipe, page 175)	
1	egg, beaten	1

1. Cook potato in boiling salted water for 15 minutes or until tender. Drain, reserving ½ cup (125 mL) water. Mash potato and set aside.

2. In a medium saucepan over medium-high heat, combine reserved potato water, ground pork, ground beef, garlic, onion, thyme, salt, pepper, sage and cloves. Bring to a boil. Reduce heat to low and simmer, uncovered, for 30 minutes or until meat is cooked through and almost all liquid is absorbed.

3. Add mashed potato to meat mixture. Mix well. Let cool.

4. Divide dough into two balls. On lightly floured surface, roll out each ball into a 12-inch (30 cm) circle. Place one circle in prepared pie plate and trim edges.

5. Pour meat mixture into bottom of pie shell. Top with remaining pastry. Trim and flute edges. Cut two slits in top for steam to escape. Brush with beaten egg. Bake in preheated oven for 30 minutes or until pastry is golden and filling is hot. Check after 20 minutes and rotate if baking unevenly.

Double-Crust Pie Pastry

MAKES ENOUGH PASTRY FOR 9-INCH (23 CM) DOUBLE-CRUST PIE

2 cups	all-purpose flour	500 mL
1/2 tsp	salt	2 mL
1/2 cup	cold butter, cubed	125 mL
1/2 cup	cold shortening, cubed	125 mL
1 tsp	vinegar	5 mL
1/2 cup	ice water (approx.)	125 mL

1. In a large bowl, combine flour and salt. Cut in butter and shortening with pastry blender or two knives until mixture resembles coarse crumbs.

2. Pour vinegar into a measuring cup. Add enough ice water to make 1/2 cup (125 mL). Gradually add to flour mixture, blending until smooth with pastry blender.

3. Wrap dough in plastic wrap and refrigerate for 20 minutes before using.

Food Processor Method:

1. Combine flour and salt in processor. Add butter and shortening and process with quick on/off pulses until pastry is consistency of coarse crumbs. Add ice water and vinegar mixture gradually, blending until smooth. Chill as directed in Step 3 above.

MAKE AHEAD

Pastry can be wrapped in plastic wrap and refrigerated for up to 2 days. Or freeze for up to 1 month.

Cheeseburger Pie

SERVES 4

Everyone will love this cheeseburger pie. And so will you when you see how simple it is to whip up.

TIP

Serve with salad for a great meal.

✦ Preheat oven to 400°F (200°C)
✦ 10-inch (25 cm) pie plate, lightly sprayed

1 tbsp	olive oil	15 mL
1	onion, chopped	1
2	cloves garlic, minced	2
1 lb	lean ground beef	500 g
½ cup	tomato juice	125 mL
1 tbsp	barbecue sauce	15 mL
1 cup	shredded Cheddar cheese	250 mL
	Salt and freshly ground black pepper, to taste	

BISCUIT DOUGH

1 cup	all-purpose flour	250 mL
2 tsp	baking powder	10 mL
¼ tsp	salt	1 mL
1½ tbsp	shortening	22 mL
⅓ to ½ cup	milk	75 to 125 mL

1. In a skillet, heat oil over medium heat. Sauté onion and garlic for 3 minutes or until softened.

2. Add ground beef and brown, breaking up meat, for 7 minutes or until no longer pink. Stir in tomato juice and barbecue sauce. Bring to a boil over medium heat. Reduce heat to medium-low and simmer for 5 minutes to allow flavors to blend. Stir in Cheddar cheese. Season with salt and pepper. Spread on bottom of prepared pie plate.

3. *Biscuit Dough:* In a medium bowl, combine flour, baking powder and salt. Using a pastry blender or two knives, cut in shortening until dough resembles coarse crumbs. Blend in milk, a little at a time, just until soft dough forms. Do not overmix.

4. Drop spoonfuls of biscuit topping over ground beef mixture. Bake in preheated oven for 10 to 12 minutes or until topping is golden brown.

Vegetarian Ground "Beef"

Microwave Vegetarian Chili

SERVES 4 TO 6

My mother-in-law, Brenda Marantz, avoids red meat, so she welcomes the versatility offered by the now widely available soy-based "hamburger" products. Vegetarian chili takes on a whole new texture and taste here. It's excellent served over brown rice.

TIP

Hot chili powder has more cayenne pepper than regular chili powder and offers more punch to this dish. If using only the regular chili powder, add ½ tsp (2 mL) or less cayenne to suit your taste buds.

◆ 10-cup (2.5 L) ceramic or glass microwave-safe casserole

2 tsp	vegetable oil	10 mL
1	onion, chopped	1
2	cloves garlic, minced	2
1	stalk celery, chopped	1
1 cup	sliced mushrooms	250 mL
1 cup	chopped zucchini	250 mL
1 cup	tomato sauce	250 mL
1	can (28 oz/796 mL) diced tomatoes, including juice	1
1	can (19 oz/540 mL) red kidney beans, drained and rinsed	1
1	can (19 oz/540 mL) chickpeas (garbanzo beans), drained and rinsed	1
1	can (12 oz/341 mL) corn kernels, drained	1
1 tbsp	chili powder	15 mL
2 tsp	Dijon mustard	10 mL
2 tsp	white vinegar	10 mL
1 tsp	hot chili powder (optional) (see Tip, left)	5 mL
1 tsp	granulated sugar	5 mL
1 tsp	salt	5 mL
1 lb	vegetarian ground beef replacement, crumbled (see Tip, page 180)	500 g
1	green bell pepper, chopped	1

1. In a microwave-safe casserole, microwave oil and onion, uncovered, on High for 2 minutes. Stir.

2. Add minced garlic and cook for 2 minutes. Add celery and cook for 2 minutes. Add mushrooms and cook for 2 minutes. Add zucchini and cook for 2 minutes.

3. Stir in tomato sauce, tomatoes with juice, kidney beans, chickpeas, corn, chili powder, Dijon, vinegar, hot chili powder, if using, sugar and salt. Cover casserole and cook for 10 minutes.

4. Add crumbled vegetarian ground beef replacement and green pepper. Stir well and cook for 10 minutes.

5. Stir again and taste to check seasonings. Cook for 10 minutes longer.

Vegetarian "Hamburger" and Noodle Casserole

SERVES 4

Many meat eaters are looking to incorporate more vegetarian meals into their weekly menus. This is a fabulous vegetarian entrée. No one will know there's not real ground beef in it!

TIP
This recipe can easily be doubled and freezes well. Freeze in an airtight container for up to 1 month. Let thaw. Heat in microwave for 20 minutes on High, stirring partway through.

✦ Preheat oven to 350°F (180°C)
✦ 8-cup (2 L) casserole

1 tbsp	olive oil, divided	15 mL
½	large Spanish onion, diced	½
2	stalks celery, diced	2
½	cabbage, sliced into ½-inch (1 cm) strips (about 3 cups/750 mL)	½
1	green bell pepper, cut into chunks	1
8 oz	mushrooms, sliced	250 g
1 lb	vegetarian ground beef replacement, crumbled (see Tip, page 180)	500 g
¼ cup	soy sauce	50 mL
2 tbsp	packed brown sugar	25 mL
8 oz	broad egg noodles, boiled and drained	250 g
	Salt and freshly ground black pepper, to taste	

1. In a nonstick skillet, heat 1 tsp (5 mL) of the oil over medium heat. Sauté onion and celery for 5 minutes or until softened. Transfer to casserole.

2. Add another 1 tsp (5 mL) of the oil to skillet and sauté cabbage until slightly browned. Add to casserole. Sauté green pepper and mushrooms until slightly brown, adding more oil as needed. Add to casserole.

3. In same lightly oiled skillet, cook crumbled vegetarian ground beef replacement, stirring and breaking up clumps, for 5 minutes or until heated through.

4. In a bowl, stir together soy sauce and brown sugar until sugar dissolves. Pour into skillet and mix well. Add to casserole along with cooked egg noodles. Season with salt and pepper.

5. Bake in preheated oven for 20 minutes or until heated through.

Vegetarian "Hamburger" Soup

This hearty low-fat soup is a meal in a bowl. Serve with crusty bread for a delectable dinner. Don't tell diners you've replaced the ground beef with a vegetarian version — they'll never know the difference!

TIP
One meat replacement soy product that is widely available is Veggie Ground Round by Yves. Look for it in refrigerated cases at major supermarkets, near the deli or produce areas.

VARIATION
Instead of homemade or canned vegetable stock, use your favorite vegetarian bouillon powder according to package directions.

1 tbsp	vegetable oil	15 mL
1	large onion, chopped	1
2	cloves garlic, minced	2
3	stalks celery, chopped	3
4	carrots, peeled and chopped	4
6 cups	vegetable stock (homemade or canned)	1.5 L
1	can (10 oz/284 mL) mushrooms, including liquid	1
1	can (28 oz/796 mL) diced tomatoes, including juice	1
1	can (10 oz/284 mL) condensed tomato soup, undiluted	1
2 cups	water	500 mL
½ cup	pearl barley	125 mL
½ cup	chopped fresh parsley	125 mL
1 lb	vegetarian beef replacement, crumbled (see Tip, left)	500 g
	Salt and freshly ground black pepper, to taste	

1. In a Dutch oven or large saucepan, heat oil over medium heat. Sauté onion for 3 minutes or until softened.

2. Add garlic, celery and carrots. Sauté for 3 minutes longer or until onions are lightly browned and vegetables are softened.

3. Add vegetable stock, mushrooms with liquid, diced tomatoes with juice, tomato soup, water, barley and parsley. Stir well. Add crumbled vegetarian ground beef replacement. Season generously with salt and pepper.

4. Increase heat to medium-high and bring to a boil. Reduce heat to low, cover and simmer, stirring occasionally, for 1 hour or until tomatoes are broken down and vegetables are tender.

Vegetarian Stuffed Green Peppers

SERVES 4

Stuffed green peppers are the quintessential comfort food — soothing homemade fare that you'll rarely see on a restaurant menu. This vegetarian version offers another option for non-meat eaters who still like the texture of ground beef.

VARIATION
Use cooked white rice instead of brown or a combination of green and red peppers, if desired.

✦ Preheat oven to 350°F (180°C)
✦ 10-cup (2.5 L) deep casserole

4	large green bell peppers	4
2 tbsp	olive oil	25 mL
1	onion, chopped	1
2	cloves garlic, minced	2
¾ cup	sliced mushrooms	175 mL
1 lb	vegetarian ground beef replacement, crumbled (see Tip, page 180)	500 g
1½ cups	cooked brown rice (about ⅓ cup/75 mL uncooked)	375 mL
1⅓ cups	canned diced tomatoes	325 mL
1	can (7½ oz/213 mL) tomato sauce	1
⅓ cup	chopped fresh parsley	75 mL
1½ tsp	Worcestershire sauce	7 mL
1 tsp	dried oregano leaves	5 mL
½ tsp	salt	2 mL
¼ tsp	freshly ground black pepper	1 mL
1⅓ cups	shredded sharp Cheddar cheese, divided	325 mL

1. Slice tops off green peppers and discard or set aside to cook alongside stuffed peppers. Discard seeds and membranes from peppers. Set aside.

2. In a large skillet, heat oil over medium heat. Sauté onion, garlic and mushrooms for 5 minutes or until softened.

3. Add crumbled vegetarian ground beef replacement to skillet and cook for 5 minutes or until heated through. Add rice, tomatoes, tomato sauce, parsley, Worcestershire sauce, oregano, salt and pepper. Reduce heat to low and simmer, covered, for 5 minutes.

4. Add 1 cup (250 mL) of the cheese and mix well. Stand peppers upright in casserole. Lightly pack in filling. Sprinkle remaining cheese on top. Any remaining filling can be spread around peppers in casserole (along with reserved pepper tops, if using). Bake in preheated oven for 30 minutes or until hot and bubbling.

Vegetarian Oriental "Meat" Balls

SERVES 4

This vegetarian take on traditional meatballs will appeal to those who don't eat red meat and to others who are looking to add more meatless menus to their repertoire. My mother-in-law, Brenda Marantz, devised this recipe to recapture the taste of meatballs — minus the meat — that she so enjoyed before becoming a vegetarian.

TIP
Gluten can be found in bulk-food or health stores. It helps to bind the vegetarian "meat" balls.

* Preheat oven to 400°F (200°C)
* Broiler pan, greased, or rimmed baking sheet, lined with foil and greased
* 10-cup (2.5 L) casserole

"MEAT" BALLS
¼ cup	dried onion flakes	50 mL
¼ cup	gluten (see Tip, left)	50 mL
2 tbsp	dry bread crumbs	25 mL
2	cloves garlic, minced	2
1 tsp	salt	5 mL
½ tsp	ground ginger	2 mL
¼ tsp	freshly ground black pepper	1 mL
1	egg white	1
2 lbs	vegetarian ground beef replacement, crumbled (see Tip, page 180)	1 kg

SAUCE
1	can (19 oz/540 mL) pineapple chunks, juice reserved	1
1	can (10 oz/284 mL) mandarin oranges, juice reserved	1
2 tbsp	cornstarch	25 mL
¼ cup	liquid honey	50 mL
2 tbsp	freshly squeezed lemon juice	25 mL
1 tbsp	soy sauce	15 mL
¼ tsp	ground ginger	1 mL
¼ tsp	garlic powder	1 mL
½ cup	sliced mushrooms	125 mL
¼ cup	chopped green bell pepper	50 mL
¼ cup	chopped red bell pepper	50 mL
	Cooked rice	

1. *"Meat" Balls:* In a large bowl, combine dried onion flakes, gluten, bread crumbs, garlic, salt, ginger, pepper and egg white. Mix well. Add crumbled vegetarian ground beef replacement. Mix well. Shape into about 40 "meat" balls, each 1½-inch (4 cm) in diameter.

2. Place on prepared broiler pan. Bake in preheated oven for 25 minutes or until browned, turning once.

3. *Sauce:* Pour reserved pineapple and mandarin juices into a medium saucepan over medium heat. Add cornstarch, stirring until dissolved. Add honey, lemon juice, soy sauce, ginger and garlic powder. Heat slowly, stirring constantly, until sauce comes to a boil. Reduce heat to low and simmer for 3 minutes or until thickened and glossy. Add pineapple chunks, mandarin orange sections and mushrooms. Mix well.

4. Reduce oven temperature to 350°F (180°C). Place "meat" balls in casserole. Pour sauce over top. Bake, covered, for 40 minutes or until hot and bubbling. Remove from oven and sprinkle green and red peppers over top. Let stand, covered, for 15 minutes. Serve over cooked rice.

MAKE AHEAD

Cook "meat" balls and sauce as directed. Refrigerate in an airtight container for up to 2 days.

Meatless Lasagna

SERVES 8

This vegetarian lasagna has the taste and texture of the meat version, with the added bonus of soy-rich vegetarian ground beef replacement.

TIP
Use skim mozzarella to lower the fat content.

VARIATION
Add ½ cup (125 mL) dry red wine to tomato sauce and simmer as directed.

+ Preheat oven to 350°F (180°C)
+ 13-by 9-inch (3 L) glass baking dish, lightly greased

1 tbsp	olive oil	15 mL
1	onion, chopped	1
2	cloves garlic, minced	2
1¼ cups	sliced fresh mushrooms	300 mL
1 lb	vegetarian ground beef replacement crumbled (see Tip, page 180)	500 g
1	can (28 oz/796 mL) tomatoes, including juice	1
1	can (7½ oz/213 mL) tomato sauce	1
1	can (5½ oz/156 mL) tomato paste	1
1½ tsp	dried oregano leaves	7 mL
1½ tsp	dried basil leaves	7 mL
2 tbsp	Worcestershire sauce	25 mL
1 tbsp	granulated sugar	15 mL
½ tsp	hot pepper flakes	2 mL
11	lasagna noodles	11
1 lb	dry pressed cottage cheese, divided	500 g
3 cups	shredded mozzarella cheese, divided	750 mL
1½ cups	freshly grated Parmesan cheese, divided	375 mL
2 cups	fresh spinach, divided	500 mL
¼	green bell pepper, sliced into rings	¼
¼	red bell pepper, sliced into rings	¼

1. In a large skillet, heat oil over medium heat. Sauté onion, garlic and mushrooms for 5 minutes or until browned.

2. Add vegetarian ground beef replacement, tomatoes with juice, tomato sauce and tomato paste. Stir in oregano, basil, Worcestershire sauce, sugar and hot pepper flakes. Reduce heat to low and simmer, uncovered, stirring occasionally and breaking up tomatoes, for 20 minutes or until tomatoes are broken down and sauce is thickened.

3. Meanwhile, in a large saucepan of boiling salted water, cook lasagna noodles for 8 to 10 minutes or until al dente. Drain and cool.

4. Line bottom of prepared baking dish with $3\frac{1}{2}$ lasagna noodles. Pour one-third of the sauce over noodles. Layer with one-third of the cottage cheese, one-third of the mozzarella, one-third of the Parmesan and half of the spinach. Repeat layers twice. Garnish with green and red pepper rings.

5. Bake in preheated oven for 40 minutes or until bubbling vigorously. Let cool for 15 minutes before serving.

Sweet-and-Sour Vegetarian "Meat" Balls

SERVES 4 TO 6

Vegetarians and meat eaters alike will love this rendition of sweet-and-sour veggie meatballs.

TIP

Serve over cooked brown rice.

♦ Preheat oven to 400°F (200°C)
♦ Broiler pan, lightly greased
♦ 10-cup (2.5 L) casserole

"MEAT" BALLS

1/3 cup	cooked brown rice	75 mL
2	egg whites	2
1/4 cup	gluten (see Tip, page 182)	50 mL
1/4 cup	chopped fresh parsley	50 mL
1/4 cup	ketchup	50 mL
3	cloves garlic, minced	3
4 tsp	dried onion flakes	20 mL
1/2 tsp	salt	2 mL
1/4 tsp	freshly ground black pepper	1 mL
2 lbs	vegetarian ground beef replacement, crumbled (see Tip, page 180)	1 kg

SAUCE

2	cans (each 28 oz/796 mL) diced tomatoes, including juice	2
1	large onion, diced	1
1 1/2 cups	ketchup	375 mL
1 cup	packed brown sugar	250 mL
3 tbsp	green sweet relish	45 mL
2 tbsp	freshly squeezed lemon juice	25 mL
	Salt and black pepper, to taste	

1. *"Meat" Balls:* In a bowl, combine rice, egg whites, gluten, parsley, ketchup, garlic, onion flakes, salt and pepper. Stir in ground beef replacement. Mix well. Shape into 40 "meat" balls, each about 1 1/2-inch (4 cm) in diameter.

2. Place on prepared broiler pan. Bake in preheated oven for 25 minutes or until browned, turning once.

3. *Sauce:* In a Dutch oven or large saucepan over medium-high heat, bring tomatoes and onion to a boil. Stir in ketchup, brown sugar, relish, lemon juice, salt and pepper. Reduce heat to low and simmer for 5 minutes or until brown sugar is dissolved.

4. Reduce oven temperature to 350°F (180°C). Transfer "meat" balls to large casserole. Pour sauce over top. Bake, covered, for 40 minutes.

National Library of Canada Cataloguing in Publication

Simon, Ilana, 1963-
        125 best ground meat recipes / Ilana Simon.

Includes index.
ISBN 0-7788-0076-8

1. Cookery (Meat) I. Title. II. Title: One hundred twenty five
best ground meat recipes.

TX749.S45 2003   641.6'6   C2003-901456-8

Index